# How to be an Outstanding Primary Middle Leader

GW00481231

OTHER TITLES FROM BLOOMSBURY EDUCATION

*How to be an Outstanding Primary School Teacher, Second Edition*
by David Dunn

*How to be an Outstanding Primary Teaching Assistant*
by Emma Davie

*Inclusion for Primary School Teachers*
by Nancy Gedge

*Lesson Planning for Primary School Teachers*
by Stephen Lockyer

*Practical Behaviour Management for Primary School Teachers*
by Tracey Lawrence

# How to be an Outstanding Primary Middle Leader

**Zoë Paramour**

BLOOMSBURY EDUCATION
LONDON OXFORD NEW YORK NEW DELHI SYDNEY

BLOOMSBURY EDUCATION
Bloomsbury Publishing Plc
50 Bedford Square, London, WC1B 3DP, UK

BLOOMSBURY, BLOOMSBURY EDUCATION and the Diana logo are trademarks
of Bloomsbury Publishing Plc

First published in Great Britain 2018

Text copyright © Zoë Paramour, 2018
Cover illustration © Ahoy There, 2018

Material from Department for Education and Ofsted reports used in this
publication are approved under an Open Government Licence: www.
nationalarchives.gov.uk/doc/open-government-licence/version/3/

Zoë Paramour has asserted her right under the Copyright, Designs and Patents
Act, 1988, to be identified as Author of this work.

Bloomsbury Publishing Plc does not have any control over, or responsibility for,
any third-party websites referred to or in this book. All internet addresses given
in this book were correct at the time of going to press. The author and publisher
regret any inconvenience caused if addresses have changed or sites have ceased
to exist, but can accept no responsibility for any such changes.

All rights reserved.
No part of this publication may be reproduced or transmitted in any form or by
any means, electronic or mechanical, including photocopying, recording, or any
information storage or retrieval system, without prior permission in writing from
the publishers.

A catalogue record for this book is available from the British Library.

ISBN:
PB: 978-1-4729-5186-1; ePDF: 978-1-4729-5187-8; ePub: 978-1-4729-5185-4

2 4 6 8 10 9 7 5 3 1 (paperback)

Typeset by Newgen KnowledgeWorks Pvt. Ltd., Chennai, India
Printed and bound by CPI Group (UK) Ltd, Croydon CR0 4YY

All papers used by Bloomsbury Publishing Plc are natural, recyclable products
from wood grown in well-managed forests. The manufacturing processes
conform to the environmental regulations of the country of origin.

To find out more about our authors and books visit www.bloomsbury.com
and sign up for our newsletters.

This book is dedicated to James, who would
have read it.

# Contents

## 11 Your calendar 147

# Acknowledgements

First and foremost, thank you to my Mum and Dad, siblings and friends for your unwavering love and support. And for not minding when I had to cancel plans to write.

Thank you to everyone at Bloomsbury, in particular thanks to my fantastic editor Hannah Marston for being the calm voice of reason and an endless source of advice and support over the last 18 months. It's been a real pleasure working with you.

This book would have been substantially lacking in content were it not for the staff and pupils of the schools I've worked in. I've learnt from all of you. So, in chronological order:

To Holly Park Primary School. A few sentences are not sufficient to thank you for everything you provided me. I was new to London when I started as an overenthusiastic NQT and you became my family (literally, in some cases). Further thanks to John Maxwell and Ann Pelham, for encouraging me to try out new ideas, to make mistakes and learn from them and to embrace new opportunities (although, in hindsight, I should have perhaps forgone the canoeing...). Holly Park gave me the start to my career that every new teacher should have and if you recognise some of the ideas and advice in this book it is because I learnt so much of it from you. Once a Holly Parker...

To the Churchfields girls. Professionally, some of the most skilled and enthusiastic teachers I've ever had the privilege of working with. Personally, some of the kindest and most loyal friends anyone could ever ask for. May we continue to share adventures, advice and cheese for years to come.

To those staff at Farnham Green who kept me going during a difficult year when the task we faced seemed completely overwhelming.

To the staff and pupils (5P!) at South Hampstead Junior School. I came to you jaded and disillusioned and you helped me fall in love with teaching all over again. Thank you.

Finally, thank you to my husband, Tim. For your advice, ideas and proofreading skills (and for providing relevant Star Wars analogies on request). Thank you for being enthusiastic enough to talk pedagogy after a long day of teaching and for making endless cups of coffee. Your love, patience and humour were the perfect antidote to my self-doubt when writing this book. Here's to our next adventure.

# Introduction: 'The Best Job in the World' – fact

If you're reading this then congratulations! You already have 'The Best Job in the World' – you're a teacher. Before I went into teaching I'd had an eclectic ~~career~~ chain of jobs. I started working at the age of 14 when I worked from 9am until 12pm every Saturday behind the counter at the Post Office that sells the non-important things. You know, cheap toys, stationery, greetings cards. From then on, I've rarely been out of work. In no particular order, I've worked in: one charity shop, two cafes, one cinema, one pest control company, one ice cream kiosk, one shoe shop, two clothes shops, one gift shop and, of course, the Post Office. I've done admin jobs, retail jobs and hospitality jobs, and none of them ever came close to giving me the job satisfaction and fulfilment that I get from teaching. Of course, it's not without its challenges; as you'll already know, teaching is bloody hard work. At times, those challenges have pushed me to my absolute limits and, at one point, I walked away from the profession all together – but I couldn't stay away.

If you've picked this book up, it is likely you are either:

**a**  considering applying for a middle leadership role (if this is you, head over to Chapter 1 for advice on choosing the right school and role);

**b**  currently working as a middle leader in a primary school;

**c**  a member of my family skim reading this book out of a sense of duty, having listened to me talk about little else for the last 18 months (Hi Mum!).

Welcome, all. And now, to start building a relationship based on trust with you, the reader, I'll start with a confession.

# Confession

This book won't tell you how to be an Outstanding middle leader with a capital 'O'. WAIT, DON'T GO! Let me explain. An Outstanding middle leader with a capital 'O' doesn't really exist. For one, the Ofsted definition of 'Outstanding' changes on roughly a four-year basis. One of Ofsted's current definitions of 'Outstanding' leadership is:

> Leaders and governors have created a culture that enables pupils and staff to excel. They are committed unwaveringly to setting high expectations for the conduct of pupils and staff. Relationships between staff and pupils are exemplary. (Ofsted, 2015)

Whilst Ofsted expectations are worth knowing, they are not how we define ourselves as teachers or school leaders. One of my previous headteachers once told me that it's important that we 'reclaim the language of Ofsted'. She explained how she uses the term 'outstanding' regularly in her school but not as shorthand for Ofsted's expectations. I liked this idea and so I have decided that it is what the title of this book is doing – reclaiming and redefining the term 'outstanding'.

Remember, *nobody* is outstanding all the time – not even David Attenborough and J. K. Rowling are outstanding all the time. You are a human being (unless I've massively misjudged my readership) and this means you'll have good days and bad days. You may even have bad weeks or bad months – but it does not mean you are bad at your job – it means you are human.

What this book *will* do is provide you with advice and practical solutions to the challenges you're likely to encounter during your time as a middle leader in a primary school – everything from having difficult conversations, writing a school improvement plan to dealing with an Ofsted inspector. (Spoiler: Ofsted inspectors are also human.) So, no, this book won't turn you into an 'Outstanding' middle leader but it will hopefully help you become a very, very good middle leader without compromising your mental or physical health. Now that sounds pretty outstanding to me.

# Who am I?

My teaching career to date has been varied and challenging. I've worked in four schools, in both the private and public sector, across two key stages, with six different headteachers, survived two Ofsted inspections, and held a variety of positions from very keen newly qualified teacher (NQT) to subject leader, phase leader and assistant headteacher. In 2015, I started documenting my thoughts and opinions about education on my blog, 'The Girl on the Piccadilly Line'. At the time, I'd just accepted an assistant headship at a three-form entry primary school in East London. The school had recently been graded 'Requires Improvement' for the second time and I was to be part of a new leadership team tasked with improving it. Professionally, it was the biggest challenge I'd ever faced, and my blog was my corner of the Internet (if the Internet has corners) for venting. It was my way of de-stressing after yet another long day. Apart from my Mum and Dad, no one read it for the first three months and that was fine – my blog was for me. But over time it started attracting more and more interest from teachers all over the country and, two years later, an email from Bloomsbury appeared in my inbox asking if I'd consider writing a book for them. After deciding 'Hell yes!' wasn't the most professional response, I politely accepted. And here we are.

I am not an expert and I have never claimed to be. If anything, the more you learn about a subject the more you realise how much more you have to learn. I don't want anyone reading this to think that I imagine myself as some sort of guru or great authority. I am a middle leader, working in a primary school, sharing what has worked for me and what hasn't. All of the challenges I outline in this book I have experienced first-hand and my advice is as much based on my successes as it is on my failures, of which there have been many!

# How to use this book

This book is a compendium of research, advice, anecdotes and practical tips that I hope will help you to be an effective *and happy* middle leader. (Being *happy* is very important and often overlooked.) You do not have to read it from cover to cover. In fact, if you're anything like me the only time you read books from cover to cover is during the summer holidays and then you'll want to read something to escape from work, not be reminded of it. This book can be dipped in and out of as and when you need it. It's here for when you're asked to produce data analysis and all you can see is a page of numbers. It's here for when you have to write your action plan, monitor what's going on in your department or report to governors. It's here for when you have to give lesson feedback or have a difficult conversation. It's here for when you get 'The Call'. Keep it on a shelf in your classroom or in the bottom of your work bag. Scribble in it, tear out the pages you find useful and annotate them, and highlight the parts that you find most relevant, but don't feel as though you have to read it from start to finish, unless you really want to.

Chapter 1 is about finding the right school for you to take on a middle leadership role – it could be the school you are already in but, if not, there's some advice on what to look for when you're making the decision about whether to move somewhere new. Once you've applied and impressed them with your application, you can also find practice interview questions (and, more importantly, answers) in this chapter.

If you've already been appointed and you're eager to get going with the task ahead, then turn straight to Chapter 2. It starts by outlining different leadership styles and approaches and goes on to break down the qualities you'll need to be an effective leader. The chapter ends with suggestions about how to build and create your vision with your team.

Leadership styles and inspiring visions are all very well but there's no getting away from the fact that paperwork will be part of your new leadership role, which is why I've included Chapter 3. The first half of this chapter deals with writing an action plan, which is likely to be one of the first tasks you are faced with as a middle leader. Following that, there is advice about how to review and write a school policy that's clear and useful to the staff.

Clear communication is essential to effective leadership – this is what Chapter 4 is all about. It starts with a whistle-stop introduction to the theory of transactional analysis and how it can be used to communicate effectively with your team. It covers everything from sending emails to chairing meetings and also gives advice on how to choose your words wisely.

Of course, it's not just your team you work with as a middle leader. You find yourself working closely alongside the senior leadership team (SLT), governors and parents, which is what Chapter 5 is all about. It offers tips for when you have to present to the governing body, advice on working and communicating with your SLT and guidance on how to juggle being the 'bridge' between the teaching staff and the management team. It ends with advice about how to work with and build good, constructive relationships with parents.

Having set out your vision, written your action plan and modelled your expectations in your own practice, the next step is to find out what the impact has been on your department – yes, it's time to do some monitoring. You may even want to do some monitoring BEFORE you write your action plan, so that you have a clearer idea of what is happening in your phase or subject. Whenever you decide to do your monitoring, Chapter 6 has everything you need. As a class teacher, you'll have been subjected to all sorts of monitoring over the years, but monitoring others is a different matter. What are you actually looking for when you observe a lesson or look in children's books? How important is assessment and progress data and what can it tell you? In this chapter, I've broken down the different areas of monitoring and take you through them step by step.

Hopefully you won't encounter too many problems from staff or other stakeholders; however if you do have to have a difficult conversation, turn to Chapter 7. In this chapter, we'll go through some real-life scenarios addressing some of the trickier situations you may find yourself in and model how to handle these conversations constructively. The sort of scenarios I'm referring to are: delivering feedback about unsuccessful lessons, working with members of staff who are struggling, dealing with an angry parent who's ranting in the school lobby and so on. As I said, hopefully you won't need to refer to this chapter too often, but it is there for when you need it.

Developing others is an important part of your role as a middle leader, whether that is staff, pupils or parents. Chapter 8 is broken down into three sections: INSETs, team teaching and mentoring. These are three tools you can use to develop members of your team. It's likely that planning and delivering an INSET will be a task you face in your first term as a middle leader and it can feel incredibly daunting. Don't panic. I've delivered enough INSETs to know that they aren't *that* bad and they can even be *whispers it* enjoyable. I'll let you be the judge of that, but this chapter will give you plenty of tips on what to do and what not to do.

You have to be pretty lucky (or make some tactical career moves) to avoid an Ofsted inspection as a middle leader. And no matter how many inspections you've been through, there is nothing like getting *that* phone call to make even the most collected and experienced leader break out in a cold sweat. Chapter 9 takes you from the moment that phone rings to the day the report is published. It includes things you need to prepare for an inspection, questions you might be asked by an inspector (and, more importantly, the answers to those questions) as well as a section on myths about Ofsted that desperately need busting.

Chapter 10 is arguably the most important chapter of the book. And that's because Chapter 10 is all about looking after *you*. None of the other things covered in any of the other chapters will be possible if you don't look after yourself. Research done by the Department for Education found that in 2016, one in ten teachers left the profession (Department for Education, 2016a). This statistic is of particular interest to me because, in 2016, I was one of the teachers who left. I had burnt out and walked away from the profession believing I would never go back. (I have since returned.) You might argue that this doesn't qualify me to write about avoiding burnout, but since I have returned to teaching I've had to approach leadership differently. I've developed strategies for managing both workload and the stress of the job. These strategies don't work every day; I still have difficult weeks, or days when I buy an Easter egg just to eat on the way home (we all do that, right?) but I do hope that this advice can help you.

Chapter 11 is a calendar of the school year. I've filled in some of the tasks you'll be faced with but, essentially, it's for you to use to plan your year and to help you spread out important deadlines and events.

## What, no teaching and learning?

It's commonplace, when writing about school leadership, to include a chapter called something like, 'Improving teaching and learning'. I haven't included that sort of chapter and for a good reason: teaching and learning is not the responsibility of one individual. Everybody in school is responsible for teaching and learning; as a school, it is our sole purpose and is the focus of every decision we make. The strategies and practices suggested in this book – mentoring, coaching, monitoring, effective communication, modelling best practice, team teaching, regular reflection – if done well and consistently, will improve teaching and learning over time.

The advice in this book has been drawn from my own experiences, interviews and conversations I've had with senior and middle leaders and research that has been done into leadership. Hopefully you will find most of it useful and relevant, although I am reminded of this Mary Schmich quote as I write: 'Advice is a form of nostalgia. Dispensing it is a way of fishing the past from the disposal, wiping it off, painting over the ugly parts and recycling it for more than it's worth.' (Schmich, 1997) You may decide that some of the advice in this book isn't relevant to you and that's OK. The one thing I can guarantee is that this book will be honest and avoid overly theoretical language, empty soundbites or patronising waffle.

One final thing before we get started. For better or worse, as a profession, we are obsessed with acronyms. We have them for everything: SPaG, SEN, EAL, CPD, INSET, PPA, PPM, SLT, NQT, RQT, SIP, SDP, SEF, G&T (both kinds) to list just a few. I will explain these terms as we go but it is inevitable that they will crop up throughout the book. If there are any you're unsure about then get yourself to the glossary at the back of the book.

Onward.

# Chapter 1
# Choosing the right school and role

If you've picked up this book because you're quietly contemplating applying for your first middle leadership role, or even your second or third leadership role, then this chapter is a good starting point. This is why we put it at the beginning of the book (they sure know what they're doing this Bloomsbury lot.) Choosing the right school is half the battle. I'd argue that it's even more important than choosing the perfect leadership role. Get the school right and the rest will fall into place. In this chapter, we'll go through some of the factors that can influence your decision, how to read between the lines of what a school is really like and, finally, a few interview tips and example questions for once you've been shortlisted for your dream job. Let's start with the basics: what is a middle leader and why would anyone want to be one?

## What is a middle leader?

Middle leader is a broad term that has slightly different meanings in different schools. They have been described as 'the engine room of the school' (Toop, 2013). They are the lynchpin between the vision set out by the SLT and what happens on the frontline – the point where the talk becomes the walk. They are the driving force behind change in the school. To sum up: middle leaders make things happen.

The areas of responsibility a middle leader can have vary hugely, from being subject specific (e.g. geography leader) to leading a phase (e.g. Key

Stage 1 (KS1) leader) or managing an area of the whole school (e.g. curriculum or assessment). Each type of role comes with its own challenges and rewards and it's likely you'll do more than one middle leadership role over the course of your career. Let's look at each of these middle leadership roles in more detail to see what they involve.

## Subject leader

According to Derek Bell and Ron Ritchie, 'The overall purpose of the subject leader is to contribute to school improvement and increase standards through the provision of high quality teaching and the best possible learning opportunities for children.' (Bell and Ritchie, 1999) At its most basic level, what this means is that, as subject leader, you are responsible for ensuring the requirements of the National Curriculum for your subject are being delivered to all children. Typical first subject leadership roles tend to focus on leading one of the foundation subjects, for example history or art, given that they aren't taught as often as maths and English. Leading a foundation subject is a great way to 'cut your teeth' and develop your leadership skills. All subjects offer similar opportunities for professional development, so the best thing you can do is choose a subject that you're genuinely interested in because you're going to be living and breathing it as a middle leader. Whilst each subject is different and comes with its own philosophies and ideas about best practice, the basic principles of subject leadership are the same regardless of the subject.

## Phase leader

Being a phase leader means you're responsible for a key stage, or in three- or four-form entry schools, a year group. Your remit may include: improving teaching, managing assessment or raising attainment. What I enjoyed most about being a phase leader was the opportunity to get to know all the children within the key stage, as I spent a lot of time teaching in their classrooms. It can be easier to implement change within a phase because you're managing fewer people than when you have responsibility for a whole-school remit, such as assessment.

## Whole-school remit

The benefit of leading a whole-school remit, such as curriculum or assessment, is that, if done successfully, you will have had a significant impact on the school. Of course, with this comes the challenge of evoking change in every classroom and managing a large number of people, each with their own ideas about how things should be done.

Whatever sort of middle leadership role you decide to go for, the tasks you will find yourself doing will be very similar:

- Supporting staff
- Planning and delivering INSET
- Monitoring
- Analysing data
- Observing lessons
- Staying up to date with the latest research and big ideas.

Each role has its own challenges and rewards and it's likely you'll have the opportunity to hold several different middle leadership positions over your career, so don't get too hung up if you're not currently leading your dream subject!

As I've said, the role is not as important as the school you're working in. You need to make sure you don't end up wearing the wrong trousers.

# The wrong trousers

At the interview for my current role, my headteacher told me that when she's recruiting she looks at the experience and qualifications of the candidates, but that she also looks for the right 'fit'. Will this person fit in at our school? Do they share our values? How will they get on with the other staff? For her, this is as important as a candidate's experience and qualifications because if a candidate isn't the right fit with the school then it isn't going to work out well for the school, the teacher or the pupils.

I've experienced not being a good fit at a school and I can confirm that my headteacher's theory is correct – it doesn't work out well for anyone. A few years ago, I found myself working at a perfectly lovely school. The staff were fantastic and many of them remain close friends to this day, but there was so much I disagreed with about how the school was run that it was never going to work. When I resigned I explained to some of the staff at the school that it was like I was trying to wear some-body else's trousers. There was nothing particularly wrong with the trou-sers themselves, as they were perfectly well made and did their job very well, but they didn't quite fit and they certainly didn't suit me.

You can be the most effective middle leader in the country but if you are unable to buy into the headteacher's vision, or if your own beliefs about education are completely at odds with the ethos of the school, then it is harder to have an impact. Obviously, a level of compromise is neces-sary in any professional working environment, so pick your battles. I've yet to work for a headteacher whose every decision I agreed with and it's unlikely that I ever will. But as long as you agree with the headteacher's vision and overall approach (basically you agree with what they want to do and how they want to do it), the rest will come out in the wash.

This is why, as I've got older, I've become more honest in job interviews. As an NQT I would say whatever I thought needed to be said to get the job: I'd promise to run netball club, teach English to parents, and walk the headteacher's dog at the weekends if I thought it would help my chances. I would try to second-guess what the school was like and make myself look like I was a good fit – even if I wasn't. There is no point in pretending to buy into the school's philosophy if you don't because both you and your SLT will end up frustrated and unhappy. If you're honest about how you work and what you value it may mean that fewer schools will appoint you, but the ones that do will be the right place for you.

## What to look for in a school

There are a number of factors to consider when choosing a school. Do you want somewhere in an inner city or somewhere more rural? Seaside town or village school? A community school, faith school, free school, private school or academy? Are you happy to commute? Do you want a school that values skills as much as knowledge or one that puts trad-itional education at the heart of its practice?

I strongly advise visiting a school before applying, particularly when you are looking for a leadership role. As an enthusiastic (read: desperate) NQT I sent off dozens of applications to schools I'd never even seen as

I just wanted a job – once I even sent off a statement with the wrong school's name written in it, which was not a good move. So, visit the school and, if possible, meet the headteacher. When I was looking for an assistant headship I had a very memorable tour from a quite formidable headteacher. She proudly announced that she'd lost her entire Early Years team the previous year and, as she told me this, she punched the air in celebration. No matter how you feel about losing a member of staff, celebrating it in front of a prospective candidate shows a worrying lack of professionalism. Other comments from that tour include, 'They call the unions whenever I set foot in the infant classrooms' and 'I'm not flexible – it's my way or the highway.' Bearing in mind this was a tour for candidates considering applying to be part of this headteacher's leadership team, I chose the highway. However, her honest, if slightly controversial, approach meant that I didn't apply for a job I would have been wholly unsuited to. Admittedly that was quite a unique situation, but it highlights my point: the right headteacher is everything. By right, I mean a headteacher with a vision you can buy into and an ethos and approach you agree with.

It will require a bit of research to find out what a school is like and, for this, you start with the website. Since 2014 it has been statutory for schools to publish specific information on their website, including Ofsted reports, policies, data, etc. Make this your first port of call. Look through the policies, newsletters and reports – it won't give you the complete picture, but you'll be able to deduce some specifics about the school. Here are some things to look out for:

- **Onsite hours dictated:** Watch out for statements such as, 'All staff must be on the premises from 8am until 5:30pm.' All schools have required working hours, but it's worth looking at how they divide it up. I always prefer to be in by 7am and out by 5pm but you have to find out what works best for you and, more importantly, find a school that will allow you to work that way.

- **Monitoring:** When you're applying for a class teacher position, it's worth looking at the school's monitoring policy because it will tell you how often you'll be subject to observations, book looks and data drops. As a middle leader, this information is doubly important because you will be both subject to monitoring and carrying it out. Try to find out how often monitoring takes place: is it termly or half-termly? Are book looks informal or formal? How much paperwork is there linked to monitoring? For example, are you going to be expected to complete weekly monitoring forms and get them back to staff? Monitoring doesn't have to mean endless paperwork, but it varies from school to school.

- **Dress code:** It's not the first thing you'd think to check but a school's dress code can be indicative of the leadership style. For example, a school that dictates the specifics of what its staff can or cannot wear is more likely to micro-manage staff. General rules, such as 'no flip-flops', are fairly typical, but requesting staff don't dye their hair particular colours is not. I know of one headteacher who tore up her school's dress code when she first got the job and explained to staff she expected them to look presentable for working in a professional environment and trusted that they knew what that meant. That's the sort of attitude I look for in a headteacher.

- **Discipline:** It is a truth universally acknowledged that a school with a consistent approach to behaviour management, centrally enforced, will be easier to work in than one where behaviour management is left entirely to the class teachers. Have a look at the school's behaviour policy and decide if this is something you'd be happy to enforce. As a middle leader, you are expected to set an example, follow policies and model best practice. This is a lot easier to do if you agree with the policies in the first place. If you don't think you can give detentions to pupils for talking in the corridor or, conversely, if you don't believe in the 'restorative justice' approach, then don't work in a school that uses these methods.

It's worth remembering that school policies get updated every few years. Have a look at the date – if a policy is more than three or four years old it could mean it's due to be updated and renewed soon. This could also mean you'll have the opportunity to help create the policy and shape what it looks like as a middle leader.

Your next step is to find the Ofsted report. A word about that. It's understandable that the Ofsted report would be one of the first things you'll find when researching a school but, remember, it is just one piece of the puzzle. Just because a school was graded 'Outstanding' does not necessarily make it an easier or happier place to work – it's all down to how the school is managed. I've worked in 'Outstanding' schools that were heavily micro-managed and made me miserable and a 'Good' school where I couldn't have been happier.

Schools can change incredibly quickly, so try not to get too bogged down with the Ofsted grade. A school that 'Requires Improvement' may simply have had a couple of years of wobbly results before their last inspection. In the current climate, schools are not allowed to remain as 'Requires Improvement' for very long so bear in mind working in a school like that will have certain pressures but, with the right team and a supportive headteacher, that shouldn't be a reason not to go for it.

Finally, have a look at the performance data. In particular, Key Stage 2 (KS2) progress and attainment data. There may be a link to this on the school website but, if not, you'll find everything you need at: www.gov.uk/school-performance-tables. In Chapter 6 I'll explain how to use data in greater depth, but at this stage in the application process you're just building a picture of the school. At the level of middle leader, a school's data needn't be a deal-breaker; don't make your decision to apply (or not apply) based on results, as results can change.

# The interview

In 2014 I went for an interview for a middle leadership role and my husband (also a teacher and school leader) offered this piece of wisdom: 'Given the current climate, you could go into that interview and say the words "impact" and "challenge" over and over again and you'd probably still get the job.' Whilst I didn't take this advice, he was making a valid point. No one likes buzzwords but we all find ourselves using them, particularly in interviews, which can sometimes feel a bit like buzzword bingo as you try to cram as many in as possible: 'quality-first teaching' – tick; 'challenge and differentiation' – tick; 'progress over time' – BINGO! Whilst it doesn't do you any harm, from someone who has sat on a number of interview panels you should know, everyone churns out the buzzwords but the candidates who are successful do more than that. Before we go into specific examples of questions, here's some general interview advice:

1  **Give examples.** 'What I did ...' is far more powerful than, 'What I would do ...', so draw on your experiences and give examples. Before you go into the interview write down EVERYTHING you did as a class teacher or middle leader in your last school. Everything from clubs you ran to assemblies and shows you wrote or directed, initiatives you implemented in your own classroom, interventions you planned and delivered for children who were falling behind, and trips you organised. Being a class teacher requires a vast number of skills and competencies – most of which are transferable to a leadership role.

   If this is the first leadership role you've applied for, you may not think you have relevant examples to draw on but, trust me, you do. In my second year of teaching I took over the task of writing the staff pantomime. It meant convincing exhausted teachers to don ridiculous costumes and summon the energy to perform enthusiastically for the pupils on the last day of the autumn term. I used this as an example of my ability to get people on board when I was applying for my first leadership role.

2  **Take your time.** When you've been asked a question, it's tempting to launch into an answer straight away, which can often result in waffling, particularly if you're nervous. So, take a minute to sit and think, 'Why are they asking this question – what do they want to know? What examples do I have of this from my experience?' It's perfectly acceptable to ask the panel if you can just take a minute – if anything it shows you're really considering the question. So, stop – think – and when you're ready, start answering.

3  **The interview is a two-way process.** This is too often forgotten. The interview is as much an opportunity for the school to impress you as it is for you to impress them. It is your chance to check that this really is the right school for you and for you to learn more about the headteacher's vision and the way they lead their school. Depending when you visited, it may be the

first time you've been to the school when there are children in, so make the most of the chance to learn as much as possible about what may potentially be your new place of work.

4   **Impact.** Whilst you shouldn't follow my husband's advice and simply repeat the word 'impact' over and over again, if you are giving an example of something you've done always finish by explaining what impact it had, e.g. 'I started a football club for the girls in my class and it had a noticeable impact on their attitude towards their learning in class. They grew in confidence and didn't let the boys talk over them in the way they had previously.'

## Interview questions

The following questions are the sort you are likely to be asked in a middle leadership interview. This list is by no means exhaustive, but it is a rough guide. So, in no particular order:

1   **Why do you want to work at our school?**

With this question, they're looking for you to show that you've done your research. What is it about their school that drew you to it? If you've visited, speak about something you saw on your visit.

'On my visit to the school it was really refreshing to see that your pupils are being offered a genuinely broad curriculum. It was the first thing that struck me. It excites me to think about what I could do as geography leader in a school that really values foundation subjects as much as maths and English.'

2   **How would you deal with a member of staff who refuses to follow a policy that you've introduced?**

Whilst it may not be worded exactly like this, you will most likely be asked a question about how you'll get people on board, in particular more reluctant members of staff.

'First of all, I would check that they'd heard and understood the policy; schools are busy places and sometimes, no matter how clear we believe we've been, new initiatives can't cut through the day-to-day tasks. So, I'd go and check the member of staff had understood what was being asked of them. I would then explain to that member of staff *why* that policy had been introduced. Do they know what we're trying to achieve? Finally, I would ask them if there was any support they felt they needed in order to implement the policy and tell them to come and find me if they were unsure or needed more support. As an absolute last resort, I would speak to the person line managing that member of staff about creating a performance management target to follow school policies but, as I said, I'd try a number of other strategies first.'

**3   Can you give us an example of a time you identified a problem and developed and implemented a solution?**

For this you could talk about identifying which pupils were falling behind by analysing the data and looking in their books and then discuss the intervention you planned to support them. Don't forget to mention the *impact* your solution had.

'After a round of assessment I identified a group of boys in my class who were falling behind in maths. I met with parents and gave them some work to do at home and designed a ten-minute intervention that I did twice a day with them. By the end of the term the gap between those boys and the rest of the class had closed and they were working at the National Expectations for their age group.'

**4   What are your strengths?**

I don't really like this question and think it's completely pointless because it tells you very little about the candidate, other than whether they know which traits are acceptable to list as a strength in a professional environment. There are a number of qualities you could choose from (because you're brilliant!) but try to choose the strengths that match the skills needed to do the job and give examples of how you have used these strengths in the past.

'I am patient, hardworking and good at getting people on board. For example, this year ...'

### 5   What are your weaknesses?

Another example of a question that tests whether you know the answer to this question. PLEASE DON'T SAY YOU'RE A PERFECTIONIST. Think of something more original. Something like, 'I'm overly critical of myself' is a safer bet. If you're really stuck, choose an area of your professional development that you believe needs work, for example, 'I need to be more confident when it comes to using new technology in the classroom.'

One of my weaknesses is that I can sometimes be quite impetuous – if there's something I want to try or introduce I'll want to get going straight away, which is fine within my own classroom but as a leader you can't rush ahead, you must keep your team with you. So, my answer to the weaknesses question is this anecdote:

'A headteacher once told me I was like the oil and the school was like a rusty bike. He said, "Zoë, you're essential for getting things off the ground and getting things moving. You have ideas and enthusiasm and you can get people on board." He then told me he considered his role was to be the brakes of the bike, so, when I'd come running into his office about to burst with excitement about an idea that I wanted to introduce, he'd be the one to say, "OK, that sounds interesting – how would it work in Early Years?" or, "What are we going to drop from the school day in order to fit that in?"'

I'm sure I've put plenty of headteachers off appointing me with this answer but my philosophy with interviews is always that the right school for me will like this answer and be happy to be my brakes.

### 6   Thank you for letting us observe your lesson – how do you think it went?

It's more than likely you've been asked to teach a lesson as part of the interview process. If you're asked to talk about how it went, it can be tempting to try to use this as an opportunity to big yourself up but the best thing you can do is reflect on it honestly. As a middle leader you'll need to develop other staff members' teaching and, to do this, you need to be able to accurately assess the quality of their teaching. So, show you can do this with your own lesson.

If it was a good lesson, explain why and give one or two things you would change if you were to teach it again. Interview lessons are rarely your best teaching, so don't be afraid of saying this! At my last interview, I said my lesson wasn't challenging enough and I'd overestimated the support they would need. I said that I thought I'd rushed through the input to make sure I got some writing out of them during the half-hour session but, really, I should have been confident that the discussion part of the lesson was valuable enough and taken my time to deliver the input properly. I got the job.

### 7    How would your colleagues describe you?

Words to use: hardworking, supportive, good humoured, organised, reliable (I often go with 'a bit of a geek' as it's my own belief that all the best teachers are geeks).

Words to avoid: messy, a good laugh, abrupt …

You get the idea – highlight the positives and play down your weaknesses.

### 8    If you were appointed, what would be your first priority?

Key first steps when taking on a middle leadership role are building relationships and finding out how the land lies: namely, what's being taught, what the strengths of your department are and what areas there are for development.

'My priority would be building relationships with pupils, staff and parents because I believe strong relationships are vital for effective leadership. At the same time, I'd want to find out exactly what was happening in (insert remit here) at the moment: how often it is taught, the strengths and weaknesses (and so on).'

### 9    What's the difference between a leader and a manager?

This is another one of those questions where you learn very little about the candidate other than their ability to regurgitate an answer they've memorised. The answer is generally a variation of the following: leaders innovate, have vision and inspire;

managers focus on systems and structures – the logistics. Ultimately to be an effective middle leader you need to be able to do both. You can give all the Mandela-style inspirational speeches you want, but teachers need to know when their playground duty is and who is covering their planning, preparation and assessment time (PPA).

**10 Is there anything you'd like to ask us?**

This is the one question I dread because apparently, you're not really allowed to just say, 'No thanks, I think I'd just like to go home, pour myself a large glass of wine and wait for your phone call.' Try to avoid a question you could easily have looked up, e.g. 'How many pupils are there in each class?' or 'What is the salary?' An open question that will give you information about the school that you can't find on the website is your best bet. Something like, 'Were I to be successful, what would be the most challenging part of my role?'

As I said, these aren't going to be the exact questions you will be asked in a middle leadership interview and I'm not for a second suggesting you memorise these answers, but hopefully this has given you some idea of the sort of questions you might face. Don't get bogged down with preparing specific answers – just make sure you have plenty of real-life examples up your sleeve and always, always remember IMPACT.

## The task

Interviews for leadership roles are likely to include a couple of tasks to complete as part of the selection process. This could be:

- Observing a lesson and feeding back
- Carrying out book scrutiny
- Analysing a set of data
- Interviewing the school council
- Writing a letter to the parents

For advice and tips on how to carry out the data task, book scrutiny or lesson observation go to Chapter 6, 'Monitoring'. If you're asked to interview the school council, this is an opportunity to show how you build relationships with pupils. If it's a small group, try to learn as many of their names as you can over the course of the interview. Ask them questions that are specific to their school and show that you've been paying attention as you've been walking around, e.g. 'I see you've been learning about British Values in assembly recently. Are these important in [insert name of school]? How do you use them?'

If you're asked to write a letter to the parents, your interviewers are looking to see if you can communicate information clearly and concisely. Your letter shouldn't be any more than three paragraphs long. Make sure you include all the key information and the name of a person the parent can contact if they require further details. It's possible the school are also looking at your spelling, grammar or even handwriting, so, like we say to the pupils, take your time, don't rush and proofread your work before handing it in!

## The call

Second only to the phone call from Ofsted, the call that can cause the most experienced and calm teacher to break out in a cold sweat is the call to tell you whether or not you've got the job. If you're not successful, don't take it to heart; the interview process takes practice like everything else. There could be a plethora of reasons as to why another candidate was successful. If you're offered feedback, accept it – most schools will be helpful and constructive and will help you learn from the experience. If you are successful, give yourself a big pat on the back and celebrate – you're a middle leader!

So, you've found your school, you've wowed them with your brilliant teaching and interesting ideas, and you've bagged your middle leadership role. Now, let's get stuck in.

# Chapter 2
# You as a leader

In September 2008 I sat in the Roger Stevens building at Leeds University listening to the first of many PGCE lectures. 'One thing I want you all to do, starting today, is to visualise yourselves as teachers,' the lecturer announced to the sea of hoodies that sat in front of her. 'There's you and then there's you as a teacher. How will you behave as a teacher? What sort of things will you say and do as a teacher? How will you dress? Visualise these things.' I'd decided at the age of ten that I was going to be a primary school teacher, so I had spent most of my life visualising it: I would wear carefully put together outfits from some high-end store, my hair would be neat and my voice would be gentle and warm (I would never shout). My classroom would be a bustling, purposeful environment that was always tidy. My pupils would absorb every bit of knowledge I imparted and would share my passion for reading. 'Please, Mrs Paramour, read us more Charles Dickens,' they'd plead (actually my current class are a bit like that – but this is rare). Essentially, I'd visualised that I'd be a mix between Miss Honey and a female version of John Keating. It is no wonder I had such a shock when I got thrown into a placement in Halton Moor later that year.

Whilst my own visualisation was hopelessly idealistic and naïve, as you embark on your next leadership role, it is worth thinking: 'What will you be like as a leader?' and 'How will you lead?'. Think back to some of the leaders you've worked with in schools; whether they were good or bad, you can learn from them. What qualities do you already have that will make you an effective leader and, most importantly, what qualities will you need to develop? We often find we can easily identify the weaknesses in the leaders we've worked for but identifying our own can be difficult. I'm talking actual weaknesses, not the sort of weaknesses you say you have in an interview situation. Mine are as follows:

- I will delay difficult conversations for longer than I should, which ultimately makes them harder to have.

- Like so many teachers, I am unwilling to drop any of the spinning plates (or even let them spin slightly slower than they should) and often end up sacrificing my health as a consequence.

- When I'm especially stressed, I can sometimes get 'tunnel vision' and find it difficult to take on other people's problems at the same time as my own, which is something you have to be able to do as a leader.

These are all weaknesses I am working on and I hope that one day they will no longer be weaknesses. Some of these things I've always known about myself and others I found out in my first leadership role. The first two in particular I am much better at than I was five years ago when I got my first leadership role, but there's still room for improvement. Take some time to reflect on your own practice: identify your weaknesses and share them with your line manager because they will be able to help you work on them. Knowing what you need to know is half the battle.

# Leadership styles

So, how do you lead? This is something that will change and evolve over your career but to begin with, let's look at some of the research on leadership styles and the pros and cons of adopting them as a middle leader.

Back in 2000, Daniel Goleman set out to define the most common leadership styles and test their efficacy. He identified the following six different leadership styles: coercive, authoritative, affiliative, democratic, pacesetting and coaching (Goleman, 2000). Before we look at the conclusions he drew from his research, let's explore each of those styles in turn.

### The coercive style

What does it look like?

Remember the 'my way or the highway' headteacher who gave me that tour when I was looking for a job in Chapter 1? That's a classic coercive leader: a leader who demands compliance from their team above all else. There is little flexibility and plenty of micro-management. Coercive leaders want things done in a specific way and are unforgiving of mistakes. They maintain their authority by threatening others or undermining them. In school leaders, coercive leadership can manifest itself as treating the adults in the school like children who are behaving badly, e.g. telling them off, reminding them of the rules, putting sanctions in place and rewarding obedience.

## What are the pros?

There is a place for this style of leadership in certain contexts. For example, if you have a school in crisis that needs turning around quickly, there is an argument for using a coercive leadership style to ensure things are done in a specific way and within the preferred timescale. Similarly, if there is a member of staff who, despite plenty of support and coaching, still refuses to get on board with a new initiative, there is sometimes a case for using a coercive style. Finally, coercive leadership is effective and necessary during an emergency, e.g. getting people out of a burning building, but, unless you're a firefighter, that hopefully isn't a daily occurrence.

## What are the cons?

The obvious downside is that, long term, coercive leadership can demoralise staff, which, in turn, has a negative effect on the pupil. Coercive leadership can lead to resentment when self-motivated, hardworking and skilled members of staff feel like they are no longer trusted to do the job they are trained to do. Secondly, as the hallmark of coercive leadership is demanding obedience from your team, another negative consequence is that it can infantilise staff and deskill them because so much of how they do their job has been decided for them. It discourages risk-taking and new ideas, which are integral to good teaching and learning.

Finally, staff can begin to lose pride in their work under a coercive leader. They start to believe that they are simply a cog in somebody else's machine and are producing little, if any, value for themselves. Of the six leadership styles that Goleman identified, there were two that were found to have an overall negative impact and the coercive leadership style is one of them.

## What sort of things might they say?

'Do as I tell you.'

'I want it done this way.'

## Example of a coercive leader

You can probably think of your own example, as these leaders tend to be quite memorable but, if you're struggling, Miss Trunchbull, from Roald Dahl's *Matilda*, is an extreme case of a coercive leader.

# The authoritative style

## What does it look like?

According to Goleman, 'vibrant enthusiasm and clear vision' are the hallmarks of an authoritative leader, which is why this leadership style is sometimes called the 'visionary style' (Goleman, 2000). These leaders decide on and set the overall goal, but allow the individuals in their team to work out how they're going to get there. This approach to leadership was once described to me as 'sketching the outline of a picture and allowing your staff to fill in the details'. It is considered a good starting point for a leader who is new to their role because it is all about sharing your vision with your team and inspiring them to follow you. This style relies heavily on charisma and the leader's ability to share their vision and get people on board.

## What are the pros?

Almost any fictional hero you can think of is an authoritative leader: from Mel Gibson's William Wallace in *Braveheart* to Whoopi Goldberg's Deloris Van Cartier in *Sister Act*. It's a popular leadership style and for good reason. The authoritative leader encourages people to think for themselves and to have their own ideas. This encourages risk-taking and innovation, and boosts staff morale. When people are clear about how their work fits into the school vision and they can see the impact they are personally having, they are more motivated. For this reason, it's a regularly used style of leadership and hopefully one you've encountered in the leaders you've worked with in the past.

## What are the cons?

The authoritative leadership style is most effective when the team share your vision – if they don't, they won't feel motivated to contribute to it.

Secondly, this style can be harder to pull off when working with a team who are more experienced than the leader, as it relies heavily on the team wanting to follow.

### What sort of things might they say?
'I'm sure you all have plenty of ideas about how best to tackle this.'
'Come with me and together we'll get there.'

### Example of an authoritative leader
Barack Obama – 'Yes we can.'

## The affiliative style

### What does it look like?
The affiliative leader puts the people in the team first and focuses on relationships and staff morale. The priority of an affiliative leader is maintaining a happy and harmonious team. They are heavy with praise and encouragement, rarely reprimand or sanction, and have huge trust in the people working for them. In schools, this leadership style is very common, as adults who choose to spend their working day with children tend to have quite a nurturing, people-orientated side to them.

### What are the pros?
An affiliative leader can provide a much-needed morale boost to staff who have recently experienced intense stress or fallout. By putting the needs of their staff first, people feel looked after and happy at work, which motivates them to work harder. Affiliative leaders are often well liked and create happy working environments. What's not to like?

### What are the cons?
As it happens, there are a few downsides to working for an affiliative leader. Firstly, by prioritising staff happiness, they can sometimes shy away from having difficult conversations that need to be had. For example, if you have a school site manager who repeatedly fails to do his job, staff will quite rightly expect this to be followed up by the leadership team and, if it isn't, will grow resentful with both the site manager and the leaders who haven't corrected his behaviour.

Part of being a leader is not being afraid to take necessary action that people might not like and accepting that you can't always please everybody. If a leader's priority is keeping people happy, it may impair their judgement when it comes to making important decisions.

## What sort of things might they say?
'What could we do to make you feel happier at work?'
'How do you feel about that idea?'

## Example of an affiliative leader
Princess Leia. After Alderaan was destroyed by the first Death Star, her title of 'Princess' no longer had any power. Her authority within the rebel alliance was based entirely on the relationships she formed with its other leaders.

## The democratic style

### What does it look like?
When I think of the democratic leadership style, I'm always reminded of this famous quote from Henry Ford (the founder of the Ford Motor Company): 'If I had asked people what they wanted, they would have said faster horses.'

Sadly, whilst researching this book, I found out that Henry Ford didn't actually say this (damn you, misleading Internet memes) but it does sum up the democratic leadership style quite nicely. A democratic leader works by collaborating with their team and bringing them into the decision-making process. They'll listen to everybody's opinions and suggestions before making a decision.

### What are the pros?
When this leadership style works well, the democratic leader gives everybody a voice, which means the team feel valued. A democratic leader can be very motivating for people, as they know their ideas are being heard. Also, two heads are better than one and there's every chance somebody in your team may have a solution to a problem you hadn't considered or an idea that could improve your department. It's a style that all leaders should use occasionally, but there are some cons to consider.

## What are the cons?

If you've ever been to an Indian restaurant with more than four people and tried to agree on side dishes, you'll know all about the flaws of sharing the decision-making process with others: it can take time and it can also lead to endless discussions that don't necessarily go anywhere and 20 minutes later you're no closer to ordering and everyone is hungry and a bit cross. The democratic leadership style can slow down important decisions and mean that people sometimes feel a bit leaderless.

Finally, school leaders make dozens of decisions every day: some minor, some major. There isn't always time to consult others and this may not lead to the best solution anyway. The phrase 'a camel is a horse designed by committee' comes to mind.

## What sort of things might they say?

'I'd like to know what you all think about this.'
'Let me know if you have any ideas.'

## Example of a democratic leader

Twitter. It was founded by four men: Jack Dorsey, Biz Stone, Evan Williams and Noah Glass. Whilst Dorsey is generally considered the original founder, the company makes decisions collaboratively, sometimes going as far as to consult users before making changes and improvements.

## The pacesetting style

## What does it look like?

The pacesetting leader makes themselves the example of how things should be done. As an assistant headteacher in a struggling school, this was my default leadership style. I was a firm believer in leading by example and not expecting my team to do anything I wasn't willing to do myself. I thought that if I made sure my books were always up to date, my displays always well-presented and relevant, and my lessons always at a standard that any one of my team could walk in at any point and learn from me, then things would improve. It wasn't because I thought I was amazing or that everyone should do things my way, it was more because I didn't believe in asking people to do things I wasn't willing to do myself. So, if the school policy was that work should be marked the same day it's done, then you could be damn sure that's what I did. If the school policy insisted that I did all my planning at 2am every Thursday, I would probably have done it because I was so determined to lead by example.

## What are the pros?

When I was an assistant headteacher, there were perhaps a few people who respected the fact I was willing to work hard and 'walk the walk' rather than just 'talk the talk'. In the past I'd found myself frustrated by SLT members who shied away from teaching but would happily dictate to others how to do the job. I was determined never to be that person.

Equally, an SLT that does no pacesetting somewhat limits what they can expect from their staff – you can't ask your staff to work harder than their leadership team. Pacesetting is a useful strategy but has to be used in partnership with other leadership strategies and styles.

In my experience, for a few, equally motivated members of staff, I believe I was able to have a positive impact with this approach. They appreciated and enjoyed having a member of the SLT on the frontline as it were. But, whilst this sort of approach to leadership can be effective on short-term, intensive projects, long term the cons start to outweigh any benefits.

## What are the cons?

Put simply, using the pacesetting style alone doesn't work. Firstly, it can lead to burnout. You CAN'T be on top of everything all the time when you're a teacher. That's just a fact. Or, you can, but it will mean 18 hours' work a day, seven days a week, and sacrificing your relationships with your friends and family and your mental and physical health in order to do it. It was my headteacher who, having found me in tears of frustration and tiredness over a pile of exercise books, pointed out the fatal flaw in my approach. 'Nobody is the perfect teacher. You're killing yourself trying to be something that doesn't exist. Nobody is expecting perfection from anyone here: least of all from a teacher who also has a demanding leadership role. Plan and deliver your lessons, mark as much as you can whilst still getting out of here at 5:30pm to have some of your evening.'

The second problem with the pacesetting leadership style is that it can make those members of your team who are struggling to keep on top of everything feel overwhelmed, inadequate and, ultimately, resentful. The message those members of staff are receiving is, 'Well, if I can do it, you should be able to do it.' It can come across as hugely arrogant and it can mean you don't stop to address the reasons why they might be struggling in the first place. It makes your team far less likely to come to you for help or be honest about the things they need support with. Worse still, in trying to keep up with your expectations they too could burn out.

And finally, as I've already mentioned, trying to keep all the balls in the air and plates spinning on sticks pushed me to my limits. When things did go wrong, or I did mess up, rather than feeling any sympathy my team were often relieved or secretly delighted. Now obviously this is because pacesetting was my default leadership style. A bit of pacesetting now and again is not a bad thing but, like most of the leadership styles, it needs to be one tool in your arsenal, not your *modus operandi*. Remember how I said there were two types of leadership that have an overall negative impact? The first was coercive; well this is the second.

## What sort of things might they say?
'Do you want to come and watch me do that?'
'What I do is ...'

## Example of a pacesetting leader
Me circa 2015/2016. Sorry, colleagues at that school. And, if you don't know me (then firstly, thank you for buying this book), then Monica Geller from *Friends* is perhaps a more relatable example of a pacesetting leader. As head chef at a restaurant, she holds herself and her team to impossibly high standards.

## The coaching style

### What does it look like?
The clue is in the name: coach. When picturing this leadership style, think about everything a sports coach does – encourages, supports, offers feedback, motivates, listens – and you have the coaching leadership style. It's a style that is less about improving your team's ability to complete specific tasks or teach in a certain way and more about their personal development. Coaching leaders ask probing questions that make members of their team reflect and improve, meanwhile providing lots of feedback and support. This leadership style is particularly appropriate in a school environment because it is essentially a type of teaching. It is all about working with staff to set long-term goals and then help them come up

with a plan to achieve them. We aren't talking about 'have 86 per cent of children achieving National Expectations by July' sort of goals. Coaching goals tend to be more personal, e.g. to develop strategies for managing stress. Interestingly, Goleman's research found that, of the six different leadership styles he identified, coaching was the one used the least often.

## What are the pros?

When it's done well, coaching leaves staff more skilled and motivated. This creates a positive working environment and helps good relationships form between the leader and the team. Happy, reflective teachers working towards their goals – surely that's the dream?

## What are the cons?

Coaching is a long-term investment and leaders have to be prepared to accept that they may never reap the rewards of that investment. This is possibly why it is one of the leadership styles that is used least often. Coaching also relies on the team member being willing and open to self-improvement. As someone who has received and delivered coaching, I can say from experience that this is not a leadership style that everybody likes. It requires a very honest and open relationship between the leader and the team, as the person being coached has to identify their own weaknesses as targets. Finally, coaching leadership is a bit like counselling in that the coach will use questions to guide their colleague to find their own solution, which I know, for some people who would rather just be told what to do, can be quite frustrating.

## What sort of things might they say?

'Why don't you try this?'

## Example of the coaching style

There are almost too many to choose from. There's Francois Pienaar, captain of the underperforming Springboks in the film *Invictus* or there's Dumbledore, who in *Harry Potter and the Half-Blood Prince,* asks Harry to reflect on why he failed a particular task: ' "And you feel that you have exerted your very best efforts in this matter, do you? That you have exercised all of your considerable ingenuity? That you have left no depth of cunning unplumbed in your quest to retrieve the memory?"' (Rowling, 2005)

In your time as a teacher, you will have worked with a variety of leaders and can probably think of your own examples for each of the different leadership styles. So which style is the most effective? As we've already discussed, the only two styles that Goleman found to have a negative impact were the coercive style and the pacesetting style. But even those two styles have their place – it's only long term they are detrimental. Like so many who have conducted research into leadership styles, following his research, Goleman concluded that, 'Many studies, including this one, have shown that the more styles a leader exhibits, the better. Leaders who have mastered four or more – especially the authoritative, democratic, affiliative, and coaching styles – have the very best climate.' (Goleman, 2000)

Good leadership means adapting your leadership style according to the situation or the person. As a middle leader you'll find that you need to learn to switch seamlessly between leadership styles depending on who you are working with or what you're working on, so this is the perfect moment to introduce you to the concept of 'situational leadership'.

# Situational leadership

Paul Hersey and Ken Blanchard (1969) developed a model called 'situational leadership'. This involves adapting your leadership style to suit what they call the 'performance readiness' of the team. Performance readiness, put simply, means the capability and willingness of your team. According to Hersey and Blanchard, your colleagues will fall into one of the following categories:

| Unwilling but able | Willing but unable |
|---|---|
| There aren't many of these people in the teaching profession, I like to think. These are the people who are perfectly competent teachers, but are unwilling to deviate from the way they've always known things to be done. They're likely to be obstructive and reluctant when new initiatives are introduced. | People who demonstrate this attitude can be supported. If someone is willing to put in the work, listen to feedback and take advice then nine times out of ten you can help them improve. With the right support, this person can quickly become 'willing and able'. |

| Willing and able | Unable and unwilling |
|---|---|
| In my experience, most teachers make fantastic colleagues and you will not find better or more supportive team players in any other profession. Hopefully 90 per cent of the people you meet in the teaching profession will fall into this category. These are skilled, capable and reflective professionals who work hard, are flexible, take on feedback and listen to new ideas. | Hopefully you won't encounter too many people like this over the course of your career. In the last eight years, I've met just one. If someone isn't able to carry out the basic requirements of their job (e.g. plan and deliver lessons, mark books) and they aren't willing to accept any help or try to improve then it's time to have a conversation about whether this is really the school (or the job) for them. |

Once you've got to know your team, return to this grid and think about which categories they roughly fall into. Obviously, people are changeable and complex and I'm not suggesting they can easily be classed under one label, but think of the grid as a guide to help you establish what sort of leadership your team will respond to. Let's consider what might work for the four types of colleague one-by-one.

## Unwilling but able

The unwilling but able teacher will probably work well with an authoritative leader, but you need to get them on board with your vision early on. How do you do this? First, listen to them. These are good teachers who know how to do their job. If they have concerns about a new initiative or change, then it is important to give them the opportunity to voice these and to listen because their concerns could be perfectly legitimate. My approach with these members of staff has always been to go to them first and say, for example, 'Hi Phil, I'm thinking about introducing this across our phase. All the evidence seems to suggest it can greatly improve comprehension skills, but I was wondering what you thought about it?' Phil will then feel like his opinion matters to you and will know he has your ear. It also allows you to hear any concerns he has about a new initiative privately and iron them out before announcing it to the rest of the team.

## Willing but unable

The willing but unable teacher requires coaching. No teacher goes into the profession to do a bad job and most are open to improving regardless of what stage of their career they are at. The hardest part of this relationship is telling a keen and enthusiastic teacher that they have to improve. However, it can be a positive conversation with a coaching and supportive approach. There is more about having difficult conversations like this and what to do when a teacher is struggling in Chapters 6 and 7.

### Willing and able

The willing and able teacher is a pleasure to work with. Essentially, they need to be left to do their job and to know that they can go to you for support if and when they need it and that, over time, you'll work with them to further develop and improve their practice. One advantage of having these people in your team is that, if they're willing, you can start preparing them for their own leadership role by taking a more democratic approach to leadership and consulting them on key decisions.

### Unwilling and unable

The bad news is there is very little you can do with the member of staff who is unwilling and unable. The good news is that they are very, very rare. On the whole, teachers are incredibly hardworking, understand what is required of them and will listen to and take onboard feedback. When you encounter a member of staff who is not willing to do even the most basic aspects of their job, it is frustrating and hugely damaging for the children they are teaching. For more advice on how to deal with a member of staff like this head to Chapter 7.

There have been several studies that are critical of situational leadership theory but I wanted to share it with you because I was introduced to it by a headteacher as a shorthand for identifying where support is needed and in what form. Only you can know if this will be helpful to you, but it's important to remember that, whilst these labels may help you to identify the support your team needs, you should be wary of labelling people permanently: people need to be given the opportunity to improve and better themselves. No one falls into one category and stays there forever.

# The qualities of an effective leader

There has been a wealth of research around leadership and the qualities and skills that make a good leader – what I've run through above hardly even scratches the surface – but I promised you that this book wouldn't be overly theoretical and would be based on my own experiences. I've worked for seven different headteachers and held a leadership position in three different schools. I've seen both brilliant and terrible examples of leadership and I have learnt from all of them. The brilliant ones were all very different: some were endlessly patient, others were short tempered, some extrovert, others introvert, but they all shared the following four key qualities.

1  **Self-awareness:** This is the cornerstone that all the other qualities will hang off: knowing and understanding yourself – namely knowing your strengths, your weaknesses, your biases and your likely emotional responses. In his book *Leadership Matters*, Andy Buck calls it 'one of the greatest challenges for every leader' (Buck, 2016). By strengths and weaknesses I don't mean, 'My PE teaching isn't good enough', but something more like, 'I take things too personally'. This is about your personality and habits. But how can you be sure you know yourself sufficiently? And what if your interpretation of yourself isn't how you come across to everybody else? Have you ever heard a recording of yourself and hated the sound of your own voice? ('I don't sound like that, do I?' you might ask a friend, nervously.) Finding out what your strengths and weaknesses are can be equally uncomfortable, but it will ultimately make you a better leader. As a middle leader you will hopefully have a skilled, emotionally intelligent SLT who can work with you on identifying your strengths and weaknesses and support you in the areas you want to develop. As a middle leader it is also your job to help your team know themselves and support them in identifying their strengths and weaknesses.

2  **Emotional intelligence:** Closely linked to self-awareness is emotional intelligence. I sometimes marvel at my headteacher's ability to remain composed under stress. Anything that's thrown at her, from the smallest problem to the biggest crisis, she approaches in the same rational, calm way. That's not to say she doesn't feel stress, I'm sure she does, but she has a remarkable ability for not letting her own stress impact on her leadership.

She's a very good example of why emotional intelligence matters in leadership. If you've worked for someone with poor emotional intelligence, you'll understand why this is one of the most important qualities a good leader possesses. There are two parts to emotional intelligence. The first is the ability to perceive, understand and manage your own emotions. The second is the ability to perceive, understand and manage the emotions of others. You cannot do one part without the other. People who are highly emotionally intelligent are able to accurately pick up on the mood of a person or a room of people; they are also open to feedback and deal with problems by communicating rather than shutting people out. If somebody has good people skills, they're likely to have high emotional intelligence. Conversely, a leader with low emotional intelligence is one who shouts at others because they're stressed, blames other people for their mistakes or lacks empathy.

3   **Fairness:** In the same way that teachers cannot show preference or favour towards any pupil (and let's face it, everyone has their favourites), a good leader treats everyone in their team fairly. I've worked in a school where staff were given preferential treatment (I've even been the recipient of it) and it does not make for a healthy working environment. I've seen members of staff dragged over hot coals for not adhering to the dress code while other members of staff saunter around in shorts. I've also seen deadlines that have been extended for some staff but not others. These may seem like small things, but if they happen often enough they will be picked up on by your staff. Of course, there will be people you feel closer to or get on better with and it's unrealistic to suggest you do not become friends with the people in your team, but your expectations have to be the same for everyone.

4   **Courage:** Perhaps now, more than ever before, being a leader in a school requires courage. In particular, the courage to stick by your decisions and convictions. In the age of social media, a decision you make is no longer just scrutinised by the rest of your team, it can become a national debate. Your decision to send a child home for not wearing the correct uniform can

make the front page on a quiet news day. As a subject leader, you may not be responsible for such decisions, but as a phase leader it's possible there are times you will be left 'in charge' when your SLT are out. But you don't just need to be brave when the *Daily Mail* are on the phone, day-by-day you need to have courage to stand up for what you believe is the right thing to do: whether that is defending a policy you've introduced or (politely) challenging a member of the SLT about a decision they've made that you disagree with. And most importantly, you need courage to take responsibility for when things go wrong.

**A little note:** remember, nobody starts off with all of these qualities; they're developed and enhanced over time. These are attributes to work towards and aspire to. Even leaders who embody most of these traits may not be like this every day. Leaders are humans: they will make mistakes, they will have bad days and they too are still learning. So go easy on yourself.

# What is your vision?

Now you've considered *how* you're going to lead your team and the qualities you need to do this successfully, you should start thinking more strategically about *where* you want to lead them and what you need to do to get there. As a middle leader, you will be expected to create a vision for your phase, subject or whole-school responsibility and deliver on this. In the first chapter, I explained how the headteacher is an important factor to consider when you are deciding where to work – in particular, whether you feel you can buy into their vision. Ultimately, everything you do as a middle leader has to be supporting that vision and working towards it. However, in order to support the whole-school vision, it is important that you have a vision and strategy for your own department, subject or responsibility too.

Put simply, your vision is the future that you want to create: how do you want your department, subject or responsibility to run and what do you want it to achieve? One way to build a clearer picture of your vision is to ask yourself this question: 'In an ideal world, what would a day in my department be like for the pupils, the staff and the parents?'

Think about how it would run, what the ethos and values would be and what it would achieve. Consider the role all stakeholders would play in your department, including governors and parents. Remember your vision is the big picture – it's the why behind what you do. The details of how you will achieve your vision will come once you've shared your vision with your team. They will help you with the detail based on their own ideas, skills and experience.

## Share your vision

Once you've got a clear idea of your vision, it's important to communicate it to your team. Most of the time leadership is about maintaining routines, keeping systems going and monitoring. Day-by-day it may not feel like you're offering inspiration, but there are opportunities to share your vision every day. You can do this at any time as a middle leader, but the start of the academic year or a new term is ideal. Call a meeting and set out your ideas for the future. It doesn't have to be lengthy (believe me, nothing kills an inspiring vision more than 32 PowerPoint slides). Something short and sweet like the following will get the ball rolling:

'My vision for our phase is a highly knowledgeable and skilled staff team working collaboratively to deliver to pupils a broad curriculum. Staff and pupils feel happy coming to school and are always looking to improve themselves. Pupils will leave our phase as independent, enthusiastic learners with the skills and knowledge necessary to thrive in secondary school. Together I'd like us to agree how we're going to achieve this and the steps that we'll all need to take to get there. This will take time – it's not going to happen overnight – but does anyone have anything they want to suggest at this point?'

So, you've established which leadership styles are most effective with your team and identified the sort of support your team require. You have a clear vision of what you want to achieve and have communicated this to your team. Next up, the nuts and bolts that will be essential for making your vision a reality. It's time to write policies and plans.

# Chapter 3
# Policies and plans

Remember that interview question from Chapter 1 about defining the difference between a leader and a manager? And how the answer to that question is that a leader inspires, encourages, motivates and sets out the vision, whereas a manager focuses on systems and structures? Well, this chapter is about the management side of the middle leadership role: the plans, paperwork and policies that it will be your responsibility to maintain and update on a regular basis.

Once you've set out your vision for your subject, phase or responsibility (as discussed in Chapter 2), policy and plan documents need to be drawn up and implemented to make that vision a reality. They ensure everybody understands what is expected of them and help keep staff on the same page. It is important to get them right, but the task of writing them can feel overwhelming at first. Luckily, this chapter is full of advice and step-by-step guidance on how to produce effective documents.

School policies tend to only get updated every few years, which means you may not be asked to write one until you are an experienced middle leader; however, there is one document you will definitely have to write and use in your first year on the job – your action plan.

## Action plan

Every subject and phase leader working in a primary school is expected to have an action plan. Your action plan outlines your priorities for the school year. These priorities may be areas you've identified as weak in your monitoring, curriculum or assessment updates that need introducing and embedding, or whole-school priorities that have been outlined in the school improvement or development plan (SIP or SDP.) Normally, the action plan is written in the first term, after a round of monitoring, or at the end of the school year in preparation for the following year. This part of the chapter will take you through everything you need to produce an action plan.

## 1. Assess where you are now

Before you start setting targets, you'll need to have a clear understanding of the strengths and weaknesses of your department. You can identify these through monitoring. Monitoring essentially means observing teaching, looking at children's work, speaking to pupils about their learning, and analysing attainment and progress data – this should give you a clear idea of what is going well and what could be improved. (Chapter 6 is dedicated to monitoring, so head there now if you want more information.)

## 2. Decide on your priorities

There may be lots of things you want to work on or introduce but try to narrow it down to three or four priorities. It could be that you need to introduce the updated curriculum or that you want to make some pedagogical changes as a result of some research you've read. At this point go and speak to your SLT and share your ideas – they'll be able to guide you and help you decide which priorities to focus on.

## 3. Turn your priorities into targets

So, you've got your priorities – fantastic! Now it's time to turn them into targets. That means turning them into specific measurable goals. For example, if your priority is 'to improve girls' reading', the target could be 'to raise girls' attainment in reading in KS2, so that 80 per cent are meeting National Expectations by July 2020'. This is a SMART target. You've probably heard of SMART targets, as schools use them a lot. What the acronym stands for changes depending on who you ask but I like to go with this definition:

**S** = Specific: Make it explicit what you want to achieve. So instead of simply 'improve reading', explain whose reading you are improving and how much you want to improve it by.

**M** = Measurable: Ensure there is a specific numerical value you can attach to the target. If it's not attainment or progress data, it could be the result of a survey, for example '70 per cent of staff say they feel that they have the knowledge and understanding to deliver the new geography curriculum'.

**A** = Ambitious: Achieving your target should improve your department. Have high expectations of yourself, your team and your pupils.

**R** = Realistic: Is this target actually achievable given the current restraints on time, budget or resources?

**T** = Time-measurable: When will this target be achieved? Try to avoid giving all your targets the same deadline. Spreading them out over the year will help you to prioritise.

After you've turned your priorities into targets, you have to confront the difficult part: working out what you need to do to achieve those targets.

## 4. Working out your next steps

Now that you've identified your starting point (where you are now) and your end point (your target), you have to work out the steps that you need to take to get from one to the other. I've always thought of the action plan as the journey between where you are and your target – every action is a step towards your final destination. For this reason, I prefer to set my plan out like a pathway like the one you can see on page 44.

Obviously the steps I've included in this diagram are overly simplified, but this should help you get an idea of the kind of steps you might need to take. Setting out my plan as a pathway and seeing each action as a step towards the target helps me focus on what I need to do. The side steps are tasks that don't necessarily lead to the target on their own but that support or enhance an individual step. How you set out your final action plan will probably be dictated by the school to fit in with their school improvement

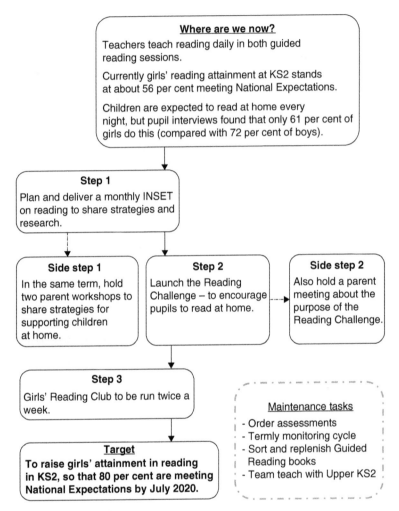

Figure: Pathway planning

plan (SIP) but, if you find this helpful, you could do this for each of your targets during the drafting stages before publishing your final plan.

## Set maintenance tasks

You'll see at the bottom of the pathway plan is a box labelled 'Maintenance tasks'; these are the things you do as a middle leader that will keep your department running smoothly. It could be anything from learning walks to team teaching or it could be those tasks you do without even thinking, such as labelling the reading books or ordering new resources. Individually, these tasks may not contribute directly to achieving the target, but it's important these tasks are on your action plan so that SLT, governors or Ofsted inspectors are made aware of what you're doing with your release time from class teaching. (Listing these tasks can also be useful for when it comes to asking for additional release time.)

## 5. Share your action plan ... and not just with your SLT

It seems to be standard practice for middle leaders to write their action plans and then email them to their SLT, who will then print them out and put them into a SIP document, which is later shared with the governors. Often the targets are shared with staff a few weeks later during an INSET, but I see no reason why your action plan can't be shared with the rest of your team at an earlier stage. If, as in the example on the plan, reading is the priority for your team and you're taking steps towards raising attainment, then the people teaching reading every day need to know what those steps are – they may even have suggestions and expertise of their own that they can contribute.

Discuss with your SLT whether it would be helpful to share the headline targets from your action plan with parents. I've seen this work successfully for some schools – parents appreciated knowing what the school was working on, particularly if the work wasn't visible straight away and it also got parents on board with the targets and encouraged them to support you to achieve them.

## 6. Reflect and review

Schools are busy places. Given that we spend most of our time dealing with children who are growing up, learning new things and changing every day, it's only natural that we spend a lot of time planning ahead. By September we're already thinking about Christmas. By Christmas we're already considering which year group we might want to work in next year. In November we start setting children's targets for July. The school year can feel a bit like a treadmill and, like a treadmill, you can be left feeling that you have to keep up with the pace or you'll fall off. Slowing down can feel difficult and stopping impossible. But sometimes you need to stop. You need to get off the treadmill and have a look at how far you've come. (The treadmill analogy falls down slightly here because on a treadmill you don't go anywhere.) The point is that you need to pause and reflect on what you've done so far and assess whether you're achieving what it is you set out to do.

With this idea in mind, it's important to put aside just half an hour each half-term to review your action plan and assess how much progress you've made towards meeting your targets. You may find it helpful to go through your action plan with somebody else, as talking about it may make things clearer. Don't worry if you haven't got quite as far as you had initially planned. Often once you start working towards a target, previously unknown obstacles emerge and you inevitably have to add a few side steps – this is absolutely fine, so just annotate your plan accordingly. As I've already explained, your action plan is a working document and will inevitably be edited and adapted over the course of the year. It's not there to be put in a plastic wallet and kept pristine. You'll probably find that by July it's covered with all sorts of scribbles, notes and annotations and that's exactly how it should look – it is there to be used.

# School policies

In my classroom there are four rules:

1  We don't talk over each other in lessons (I don't talk over them, they don't talk over me and they don't talk over each other).

2  We are honest.

3  We work hard.

4  We treat one another with respect (this encompasses all manner of behaviours from not being late to being careful with our words).

These four rules cover all possible misdemeanours without explicitly listing them. On the first day of the school year I explain to my class that I only have four simple rules and everyone can remember four rules, so there is absolutely no excuse for not following them. I've always found that having a few concise rules is more effective than having an extensive list that covers dozens of different scenarios and behaviours. The class remember them, they refer to them and they follow them. These four simple rules make our day to day run more smoothly – which is the point of having rules in the first place. When it comes to writing school policies, I take a similar approach.

School policies are the set of documents agreed by the staff and the governors that provide rules and guidance for the running of the school. They should contain the official 'party line' on the protocols and practices in your school. However, having been 'the new person' in four different schools, I know from personal experience that school policies are often earnestly distributed and read through on the first day of term and then banished to the back of a cupboard or the bottom of a bag throughout the year before being binned and replaced the following September. Occasionally someone may be heard asking, 'What's our policy on that?', only to be answered with blank looks and shrugs. This is not a reflection on the professionalism of staff at those schools; it's just that policies have a tendency to be long-winded and overly complicated, which means that they end up not being used.

School policies are reviewed and updated every three to four years. They're ratified by a committee of staff, parents and governors or, if it's a statutory policy such as safeguarding, by the full governing body. As a middle leader, it is likely you'll be asked to contribute towards or even write the policy for your subject, phase or area of responsibility. But what does a good policy look like? What will it need to include? And how on earth do you ensure people refer to it and use it in their practice? A policy that isn't used isn't just a waste of paper and your precious time; it can actually be detrimental to a school during an Ofsted inspection. Here are some tips for getting this right.

## Find out what the current policy is

It sounds blindingly obvious, but your first port of call should be the current policy. Find it, read it and highlight the bits you definitely want to keep. Check the date on the front. If the policy is only a couple of years old then it may only need tweaking – don't make unnecessary work for yourself.

## Find out what is and isn't working

Start by asking the rest of the staff what they know about and think of the current policy. The answers you receive will tell you if the policy is currently being followed. This isn't a witch-hunt – you aren't trying to catch staff out for not knowing or following the policy. However, if you're faced with blank looks or you discover that the Year 3 teachers are following the policy to the letter but the Year 5 teachers all suddenly have to check their emails, you'll recognise the parts of the policy that need a bit of work.

There are many reasons why the policy might not be being followed that have nothing to do with the staff not being compliant. Here are some of them:

1   **The policy is too long:** I once did a few days' supply teaching at an average-sized primary school and was handed a 'Teaching and learning in KS2' policy that was *34 pages* long. And that was *just* for KS2. There was a separate policy for KS1. I didn't even attempt to read it. I smiled politely, made some lame joke about a spot of light bedtime reading and then shoved it in my bag, which is where it stayed until I binned it at the end of the week.

2   **The policy is too complicated:** Keep policies simple and concise. You don't need to outline every potential scenario with detailed instructions about how the staff should respond. Teachers are skilled professionals; they can be trusted to use their own judgement so don't overload your policy with unnecessary detail.

3   **The policy has not been frequently shared with staff:** Some policies are great, but if they aren't communicated to staff on a regular basis, they might not be being followed. With regular staff turnover it's not enough to share something once at a staff meeting because staff leave, or priorities change, and things get forgotten. So, regularly communicate the key messages of the policy at staff training, meetings and feedback sessions. When new staff join, take them through the policy in a meeting – don't just ask them to read it in their own time because they won't ever make the time to do this.

**4   The policy isn't workable:** Some policies create additional work for teachers and are simply not manageable. Teachers are incredibly busy people and will prioritise the things they need to do to keep their class running. Anything beyond planning, teaching and giving feedback will have to wait.

You don't have to guess how effective your current policy is or what its strengths and weaknesses are. Ask the people who have to use it – they'll tell you what's working and what isn't.

## Consult others

Given that everyone will have to follow the policy, it is a good idea to get their input when you're putting it together. Speak to teachers, support staff and SLT, and ask them what they think the policy should include. Once you've started forming your policy, show it to them and get their feedback. You're not going to be able to change it to include every single person's suggestions, but if people feel like they've been included in the process they are more likely to take ownership of the policy and make it work.

Schools can be quite insular places, so it's worth having a look at other schools' policies too. Most schools post their policies on their website, so a quick Google search should bring up plenty of policies. A word of warning: what works in one school won't necessarily work in yours, so try to avoid the temptation to copy and paste. Your policy should be unique. My husband was once sent a link to a school website that had used a policy he wrote – it even still had the name of his school on the top!

## Be concise and clear

I once worked for a headteacher who would say that non-statutory policies did not need to be longer than two sides of A4. This may seem a little severe and it wasn't always possible, but it challenged me to be concise and to think about exactly what needed to be written in the policy. Keep your language simple and your points clear – now is not the time to show off your flair for creative writing.

Break your policy into clearly labelled subsections. On page 50 is an extract from a teaching and learning policy I wrote as a middle leader. Feel free to use this as a starting point for your own.

| Teaching and Learning at North London Primary School | Start your policy with a sentence that outlines the purpose of the policy. |
| --- | --- |
| The purpose of this policy is to outline the aims and expectations that underpin teaching and learning at North London Primary School. | *In this section outline what the aims of teaching and learning are in your school. There may be more than one (but try to have no more than five).* |
| **Aims:** To offer a broad and balanced curriculum, which equips pupils with the knowledge and skills they need to lead happy, successful lives. | |
| **Teaching:** Teachers at North London Primary School are expected to: | *The rest of your policy should explain how you set out to achieve these aims through teaching and learning.* |
| • Have secure subject knowledge and remain up to date with the changes and developments in the National Curriculum • Plan and deliver age-appropriate lessons that cover the objectives of the National Curriculum • Provide children with the verbal or written feedback they need to make progress • Work with support staff, parents, governors and external agencies for the benefit of pupils | *Under each subheading write just a few bullet points outlining the expectations. You get the idea: simple language, concise sentences and most importantly, not written in Comic Sans (one of the problems that's never really spoken about in education is the number of policies written in Comic Sans.)* |

Figure: An extract from a teaching and learning policy

## Share your policy

Once you have written your policy and are happy with it, share your policy with the staff. Begin by explaining why you've written it. Simon Sinek, author of *Start With Why*, says, 'People don't buy what you do; they buy why you do it. And what you do simply proves what you believe.' (Sinek, 2011) Keep this in mind when you're introducing your policy and explain why you've made the changes you have. For example, 'From what you said about the previous policy, X wasn't working so I've taken that out completely.' If you have made quite radical changes, make sure you explain them clearly and remember that some staff may feel anxious about these changes. Stay positive and keep coming back to why you've made these changes. Allow staff to ask questions as you go.

## Use your policy

As a middle leader you are expected to model best practice for your team and, in this case, it is particularly important. For example, if you have written a new calculation policy, it should be evident that you're using it in your lessons and books too. This serves two purposes: it tests whether your policy is workable (and will bring to your attention any tweaks that may need to be made) and it enables you to empathise with and support staff who lack confidence because they will be able to come to you and watch you using the new calculation methods. You may also want to team teach with teachers when they are getting to grips with new policies.

## Monitor and feedback

Next comes monitoring. (Chapter 6 is dedicated entirely to monitoring so I'm not going to go into it in any great length here.) Give staff time to get to grips with the new policy and then do some light monitoring, e.g. learning walks or drop-ins. Keep it low key – don't stay for too long. Just spend some time in each classroom to find out how the policy is being used. You don't need to offer individual feedback (unless staff really want it); sum up the key points and feed back to everyone at the next staff meeting. It's also important to take staff feedback, so, after a month, ask them how things are going with the new policy. Do they think it is working? Does anything need changing? Resist the urge to continuously tweak your policy – try to leave it at least six months before making any further changes. The most important thing you can do is monitor and support the staff who need it, check the policy is being used and judge the impact it is having.

Those are the two key documents that will guide you through the academic year. This chapter was about the managerial side of your role, but the next chapter is going to require you to be both a manager and a leader. It's about managing the relationships in your team.

# Chapter 4
# Communicating with your team

Have you ever worked with someone who you could never say no to? Or had a boss who, despite your best efforts, always criticised your work and made you feel that you were incapable? What about the boss who never listened? Are there people at work who make you feel you are stuck in a cycle of negative behaviour? If you found yourself nodding to any one of these questions, then this chapter will be of interest. This chapter is about the theory of transactional analysis, which is a behavioural model that helps explain why some relationships work and others don't. As a middle leader, I've found transactional analysis a useful tool for managing relationships and maintaining a positive, effective working environment. But I'm getting ahead of myself; let's start at the very beginning.

## Transactional analysis

The theory of transactional analysis is built on three philosophical assumptions that are accepted as true:

1  People are 'OK'. This means that everybody has the right to their place in the world and a right to be accepted.
2  Everybody has the ability to think for themselves.
3  People decide their own destiny through the decisions they make. Their destiny can be changed. (Berne, 1961)

The theory suggests that there are three different ego states that humans shift fluidly between: the parent, the adult and the child. These states are a pattern of behaviours, feelings and attitudes that we all operate in. It's worth pointing out that the ego state we operate in by default has nothing to do with our age – you can be 85 years old and still be led by your child ego state.

There have been years of research done into transactional analysis and ego states but the theory was pioneered by psychiatrist Eric Berne. In *Transactional Analysis in Psychotherapy: A Systematic Individual and Social Psychiatry*, Berne describes treating a male patient, a 35-year-old lawyer. During one of his early sessions the patient says, 'I'm not really a lawyer; I'm just a little boy.' Outside of his sessions with Berne this man was, by all accounts, a very successful lawyer, but in his therapy sessions he would often ask Berne if he was speaking to the lawyer or the little boy. Berne labelled these two states the adult and the child. He later identified and named a third state, when he saw behaviour in his client that appeared to be the behaviour copied from his parents. This is called the parent state (Berne, 1961).

## The three ego states

### The parent state

When we are in the parent state, our thoughts, behaviour and feelings imitate those of our parents or other adults in authority. The language and behaviour of the parent state reflect the values and judgements that were communicated to us by parents or adults when we were a child, whether that was shouting, questioning, criticising or even sympathising. They'll use phrases and expressions such as, 'Under no circumstances should anyone …' and, 'Don't do that!' This is sometimes referred to as the taught state, as it is learnt from other people at an age when we haven't developed the skills to think for ourselves (most parent-state behaviour is learnt between birth and the age of five).

The parent state divides into two further categories: the nurturing parent and the critical parent. The nurturing parent is caring and shows concern for others – they'll act in a maternal way and try to sort out everyone's problems for them. The critical parent judges and manipulates people into doing what they want through intimidation and by undermining them.

Let's look at an example. Most schools have a rule stating that pupils cannot stand on chairs and tables. (Trust me, you do, it will be under 'Working at height' in your health and safety policy.) It's a sensible policy to protect staff from having accidents and to protect the school from litigation. However, the reality is that teachers stand on tables all the time to put up displays. The school leader in the critical parent state might walk past and, seeing the member of staff stood on a table, say, 'What on EARTH do you think you're doing? Get down at once!' In comparison, the leader in the nurturing parent state would express concern for their safety, 'Be careful, that doesn't look very safe and I wouldn't want you to get hurt. Here, let me help you get down.'

## The child state

The child state is based on our internal responses to events that occurred between birth and the age of five. Put simply, when in the child state you think, feel and behave as you did when you were a young child – which is to say that you are led almost entirely by your feelings and emotions. For example, pouting or crying in response to negative feedback or criticism would be an example of child-state behaviour. The child state can be further divided into subcategories: the free child and the adapted child. The adapted child changes their behaviour following an interaction with a parent ego in order to please or appease the parent. The free child has rebelled against the parent and does whatever they want.

Let's look at an example. If your manager comes to tell you that it's been noticed you've been getting in late a lot recently, the adapted child would feel embarrassed and would make an extra effort to be in early the next day in order to please the manager and to gain their approval. The free child would shrug and turn up at whatever time they felt like the next day.

## The adult state

In his book *Counselling for Toads*, Robert de Board writes:

> '[Toad said,] "Recently I've been thinking that there ought to be another ego state, in which you are neither behaving like your parents nor feeling like a child. One in which you are more grown up. More like yourself in the present moment."'

If you're interested in transactional analysis, this is a fantastic book. It's based on the premise that Toad from *The Wind in the Willows* agrees to go to counselling after one of his friends holds an intervention following one of his many reckless stunts. Heron, his counsellor, uses the theory of transactional analysis to help Toad understand his behaviour and learn to take responsibility for it. He starts by introducing Toad to his child and parent states, then, after a number of weeks, Toad discovers the adult state for himself.

When we are in the adult state we are very much in the moment: our opinions are formed by making a judgement about the information we have at the time. The adult state is objective, rational, reflective and respectful. If the parent state is taught then the adult state is often referred to as thought. The adult is self-aware in a way that the child and parent are not. For this reason it is the only state that does not break down into further subcategories.

## Why is this relevant?

Now, I know what you're thinking, 'This is all very interesting, but what has any of this got to do with being a middle leader in a primary school? I thought you said you weren't going to be too theoretical. You promised me practical, no-nonsense tips that I could apply to my own practice.' And you make an excellent point. So how can we apply transactional analysis to leading a team? Transactional analysis was quite popular in schools in the early noughties. At that time, the emphasis was on applying the theory of ego states to the pupils to help staff manage their behaviour more successfully. However, it is often overlooked that Berne's theory can be used to manage adult relationships as a leader.

As I said, we often switch ego states in response to events and people. This can happen quickly – even over the course of a single two-minute interaction. Two people could start a conversation adult-to-adult but, over the course of the conversation, they quickly find themselves slipping into child-to-parent or child-to-child. Have a look at the conversation below between a headteacher and a member of staff. The ego states are indicated in brackets.

Headteacher: Hi Andrea, thanks for popping in to see me. (Adult)

Andrea: No problem. What was it you wanted to discuss? (Adult)

Headteacher: It's your reports. I'm incredibly disappointed –
I expected more from you. They are poorly worded, littered with
typos and you've clearly cut and pasted huge chunks of them.
What were you thinking handing them in to me in this state?
(Critical parent)

Andrea: Oh. I didn't realise. I'm sorry. I'll change them right away.
I'm really very sorry. (Adaptive child)

In this example, the conversation started adult-to-adult and then very
quickly slid into parent-child. The parent addressed the other person
as the child and the person responded as the child. The needs of the
parent ego were satisfied by the child, who adapted their behaviour as a
response to criticism. This is what Berne called a complementary trans-
action. It is complementary because the ego state that was addressed was
the one that responded. This doesn't mean it is a healthy mode to operate
in. If one person always plays the parent and the other always plays the
child in a relationship, then the child may start to feel resentful or they
may come to rely on the parent and become unable to make decisions
for themselves.

According to Berne, conflict arises when the ego state that is
addressed is not the one that responds. For example, if the parent ego
state addresses the child ego state and is met with either the adult or
parent, this will cause conflict. For example, let's go back to Andrea and
the headteacher:

Headteacher: Hi Andrea, thanks for popping in to see me. (Adult)

Andrea: No problem. What was it you wanted to discuss? (Adult)

Headteacher: It's your reports. I'm incredibly disappointed –
I expected more from you. They are poorly worded, littered with
typos and you've clearly cut and pasted huge chunks of them.
What were you thinking handing them in to me in this state?
(Critical parent)

Andrea: Excuse me? How DARE you talk to me like that? I worked
on those reports for three weeks. You might not be happy with
them, but that doesn't give you the right to pull me in and talk to
me like that. You should be ashamed of yourself! (Critical parent)

Suddenly there is a conflict as the parent addressing the child has been met with another parent. Berne calls this a crossed interaction. Crossed interactions are how conflict arises.

Half a chapter really isn't enough to unpack transactional analysis in full detail and, if that's what you're after, many people have written extensively on the theory (see the recommended reading list on page 155). But I wanted to provide a basic understanding of the ego states before we looked at how this could be applied to your role as a middle leader. It should be no surprise to you to hear that adult-to-adult relationships are the healthiest and most productive. This is what you should be working towards within your team. However, it's easier said than done because it's not just about you making sure you're always functioning in the adult ego state, it's about encouraging the rest of your team to do so too.

In management, the most common pitfall leaders should be aware of is falling into a parent-child relationship with the people they lead. The following are the signs to look out for.

## Finding it difficult to delegate

'If you want something done right, do it yourself' is the mantra of the parent leader. They find it hard to trust other people to carry out tasks as effectively as they would do themselves, so they tend to avoid delegating. On the rare occasions they do delegate they will hover around or check in regularly to see how things are going. They might drop in 'helpful' comments, such as, 'Oh, you're doing it that way? I've always found it better to do it like this.' They may even go as far as to delegate the task and then take it back a few days later, 'You know what? It might just be easier if I do it. Then you don't have to worry about it.'

## Withholding information as a way of asserting authority

Now obviously, as a middle leader, you will be privy to information that you might not be able to share. For example, it's common for middle and senior leaders to know which year groups each teacher will be working with the following academic year before it is officially announced to staff. However, there is a difference between not sharing information and making your team aware that you have information they want but are not going to give it to them. I knew a leader like this; she'd bounce into the staffroom and announce with a grin, 'We've just decided who is teaching which year group. I'm not allowed to tell anyone, but everyone is so desperate to know.' The message she was putting out was, 'I'm senior, so I'm privy to information you are not and I want to remind you all of that.' The parent leader will want their team to know that they know things that the team can't be told.

## They don't ask – they tell

'Have this back to me by Monday.'

'Don't do it like that – let me show you.'

'You're covering this class tomorrow.'

Judging when to ask and when to tell is a skill all leaders have to develop. Telling is the default of the parent leader. In their mind, they know what is best, so they don't need anybody else's opinion and they don't want to have a discussion about it.

## They try to make everyone happy

The previous three behaviours were from the critical parent. The nurturing parent will try to please everybody, which is near impossible as a leader.

There are times when every leader will need to draw on their parent ego state but in the long term it is not a healthy or effective way of managing staff. So, how do we create a team that has adult-to-adult relationships? What does that look like in practice?

# How to keep relationships adult-to-adult

Ultimately adult-to-adult relationships come down to being fair, honest and consistent. It means you treat all staff with the respect they deserve. These relationships take time and need to be worked on constantly but here are some things you can do to help:

- When setting deadlines with a member of your team, ask them, 'When do you think you could have this done by?' By asking and not telling, you're acknowledging that you are adding to their workload and, by asking them to set their own deadline, you're showing that you know they are best positioned to manage their time. Interestingly, you may find that, as a result of being given control over their own deadline, the person will volunteer a deadline that was far tighter than anything you'd have suggested!

- Present and respond to evidence. Being a leader means having to accept inconvenient truths and answer difficult questions – no matter how uncomfortable they are. Ask for evidence from your team when they want to make changes and make sure you assess any evidence carefully before making your decision.

- Be aware of your emotions and control them. Being in control of your emotions is not the same as being devoid of emotion – it just means making sure you are not being ruled by your emotional responses. For example, if you are told by the headteacher that the children in your phase or subject aren't making satisfactory progress, make sure your response is rational – ask them what the evidence is for that and ask to see it.

- When you want a member of your team to take on some additional responsibilities or solve a particular issue, don't go to them with the task – present them with an objective that needs achieving and together have the conversation about how best to tackle it. 'I'm worried about progress in reading in Year 5. What are your thoughts? What could we do about it?' This is a better approach than, 'The progress in reading in Year 5 is too slow. I want you to go and observe how KS2 teachers teach reading and write up an action plan for me by the end of next week.' It could be that the member of staff suggests a similar course of action to the one you would have put to them, but let them suggest it and discuss it together.

The one quality that separates the adult ego state from the child or the parent is self-awareness. Know your strengths, weaknesses and what sort of interactions and events might cause you to slide into your parent or child ego state.

As I was writing this chapter, my headteacher asked how it was coming along and I explained that I was writing about transactional analysis and how healthy working environments are where relationships are kept adult-to adult. This is something I believe that my school is very good at: people are treated like grown-ups. My headteacher explained that adult-to-adult relationships are important to her for a number of reasons, but particularly because she wants the children to see adult-to-adult relationships being modelled. Our pupils don't just look to us to teach them how to solve quadratic equations and write complex sentences. They look to us to learn how to interact with others, how to discuss ideas, how to lead, how to work together. So, it's important that they see healthy, and honest, effective working relationships.

## The power of words

We've already explored how the conversations we have can cause a shift in the dynamics of the relationship. Here are some handy phrases to have up your sleeve when talking to your team that will keep your interactions adult-to-adult.

### Using 'and' not 'but'

We've all sat and listened to feedback knowing there was a 'but' coming. You nod along to the positive feedback and wait for it. The second we hear 'but' it negates the positive things we've just been told. So rather than, 'Your behaviour management is great, but you really need to work on your subject knowledge in history', you say, 'Your behaviour management is great and, once you've built up your subject knowledge in history, those lessons will be much stronger.'

### Using 'at the same time'

'That's true, there is so much pressure on schools to get their pupils through these tests. We need to make sure we aren't spending too much time teaching to the test; at the same time, of course, when Ofsted come in they are going to make a judgement partly based on this data and we want all of our hard work to be recognised.'

### The language of change

When you're introducing a new system or initiative you always risk getting a response such as, 'We've always done it this way – why change it?' This response can be elegantly side-stepped if you reference that the system is going to be different to how it was done in the past. Two phrases will help you to assert this: 'Up until now' and 'In the past we have …'. For example, 'Up until now our reward system has been house points for behaviour and stickers for work. What I'm proposing is that from next term we stop using stickers and reward children's work with …'. By acknowledging how things have been done in the past, you've removed it as a potential argument. If people want to defend the status quo they now have to give a specific reason.

# Communication

Keeping relationships adult-to-adult is a good starting point for effective communication but it's very much the starting point. Your communication, from the emails you send to the meetings you hold, needs to be clear and consistent. These are the nuts and bolts of the job – the things you never receive thanks for doing, but will receive plenty of complaints about if you get wrong. Think about the duck that paddles furiously and yet from the surface looks as though it is gliding effortlessly – you want this aspect of leadership to run like that. Nobody will see the work that goes in to running a meeting or keeping people up to date via email, but they will notice when things are not running smoothly. Let's start with meetings.

## Managing meetings

Like marking, writing reports and playground duty in January, meetings are unavoidable in this job. Middle leaders are rarely taught how to lead meetings and yet getting it wrong is a sure-fire way to waste everybody's time and annoy your team. We can all think of examples of bad practice: meetings that roll on for so long that everyone switches off knowing that the time could be put to better use; meetings that could have been summed up in a three-sentence email; or, the worst kind of all, meetings for the sake of meetings even when there is nothing to say ('I know there's nothing to discuss but we always meet at 4pm on Tuesday so that's what we're going to do.'). We know all too well what bad practice looks like, but what about good practice? I once worked for a very sensible headteacher who would cap our SLT meetings to one hour and if they finished earlier then we all went home earlier. Knowing this was the case, everybody kept their contributions brief and, when there was a decision to be made, it was made quickly. There was no sense of trying to fill the time.

As a middle leader you will attend meetings with the SLT, governors and teachers, as well as chairing meetings yourself. Here are some tips for making sure the meetings you lead are positive, productive and efficient.

## Why are you calling this meeting?

It sounds obvious, but it's a question worth asking yourself before you send out the calendar invite. If you're passing on messages, could this be done in a short email instead? Or if you find yourself having a long meeting with your team each month, would it make sense to meet weekly for ten or 15 minutes instead? As a phase leader I held a weekly meeting the morning after our SLT meeting to feed back any key points and check in with everyone. The meeting was never longer than ten minutes and took place before school, which meant it couldn't overrun. If there was nothing to pass on from SLT I'd cancel the meeting and instead pop in on people over the course of the week to check in with them one-to-one.

## Create an agenda

Even if you have just two items, write an agenda and send it out to your team before the meeting and give them the opportunity to add anything they want to. Then send the finalised agenda. When you're putting the agenda together put down how long each item should take – it's helpful for people to know how much of their time they're going to have to give up.

## Keep to time

Once you've written the agenda and decided on the timings, stick to it! I think I've written this sentence a dozen times already but ... teachers' free time is incredibly valuable so show them the respect they deserve by sticking to time. That meeting may not be the last thing your team have to do before they can go home. They probably have marking to do, they might want to do some planning, or maybe they just want to get home and try to relax. So, don't allow any one item on the agenda to go on for longer than the planned time – your team will thank you for it.

## Make a decision

There's nothing worse than sitting in a meeting for an hour only to feel like you haven't got any closer to making a decision. As the leader of the team at some point you just have to call it. Even if the decision is that you will take some time to think about it and have an answer for everyone by a specific date – but make sure you set the date and stick to it.

## Keep minutes

Minutes are a written record of what was said in the meeting. They are a useful reminder of what was agreed and are also useful for holding people to account. For example, 'At the last meeting you said you'd have this ready for everyone by Friday 8th – how is it coming along?' Typically, the person minuting the meeting is not the same as the person leading, so delegate the job to a willing member of your team. After the meeting, the minutes should be emailed out to all who attended.

## Keep it positive

It's important to take feedback from your team and give them time to vent or voice frustrations but try to avoid allowing weekly meetings to become weekly moaning sessions. It will bring everyone down and eat away at morale. If necessary, you can say, 'Perhaps you and I can meet about this separately as you obviously feel very strongly about it. We haven't got the time to spend on it right now as everyone needs to get back to class.' Try to end the meeting on a positive note by thanking everybody for their hard work and offering some words of encouragement for the day or week ahead.

## Emails

As I've said, a meeting is not always necessary. Sometimes, when you just need to pass over some key information, an email will suffice, but here are some important things to bear in mind before hitting send.

Before you sit down to write an email to a member of staff ask yourself: would this message be better delivered face-to-face? If it is to just one person, would it be better to take a walk to their classroom and speak to them? This serves several purposes. Firstly, face-to-face interactions are more personal. While popping into a colleague's classroom to speak to them, you can also ask them about their weekend and find out how they're doing. You don't need to be there for any longer than five minutes, but over time it will make all the difference. Secondly, the staff and pupils will see you around school more often. School leaders are often accused of being cooped up in their offices, hunched over computers, so take every opportunity possible to walk around school, engaging with pupils and staff, and be more visible.

Obviously not all emails are better delivered in person, especially if you're emailing multiple people or have a lot of dates and deadlines you want staff to remember. When an email is necessary, here's my advice.

## Keep it brief
Anyone who's ever received a work email from me will baulk at my hypocrisy – my emails are never brief, but I am working on it.

## Highlight the key information
Set key information such as dates, times and locations in bold. That way, if somebody has forgotten the details they can just open up the email and find the information they need immediately.

## Think about *when* you send the email
This is a lesson I've learnt since working in my current school. We have a 'no emails at weekends, evenings or holidays' rule. Advances in technology have meant that we are always available, even if we don't want to be. I used to send a lot of emails on a Sunday afternoon, which is when I'd do most of my school work. I'd always say cheerfully to the staff in my team, 'Don't worry, just because I send emails on Sunday afternoon doesn't mean I expect you to read them then.' But that isn't good enough. For many people, their work emails appear on their mobiles or desktop, so, even if they don't read it, they know it's there waiting for them – it's an intrusion on their free time and a barrier to achieving a work–life balance. Try to avoid doing this if you can. I now only ever send emails on weekdays between 8am and 6pm. If you want to take your time composing the email on Sunday afternoon, that's fine, but leave it in your drafts until Monday morning.

## Follow up
Check that people have read your email. You can do this on an individual basis by asking people when you see them or doing a quick shout-out in

your staff briefing: 'Hi everyone, I've sent an email about the next round of monitoring. Can you make sure you've read it and have made a note of the key dates? Thanks.'

In this chapter we've covered how to communicate effectively with your team. The staff in your team are, however, not the only people you'll work with as a middle leader – you'll also work with senior leaders, governors and parents. The next chapter will take you through how to be the bridge between teaching staff and the SLT, and how to maintain positive relationships with stakeholders.

# Chapter 5
# Leading from the middle

Effective communication with your team is a key component of your job. However, being a middle leader means that, while you are managing others, others are managing you. This chapter deals with working with the SLT, the governing body and the parents of your pupils. The dynamics of these relationships may differ, but regular, honest and clear communication is the key to all three.

## Who are your senior leadership team?

Throughout this book there are references to the senior leadership team (SLT). However, the term SLT can have different meanings in different contexts. In my career I've worked under seven different SLTs and have been a part of two of them. The structure, hierarchy and division of labour varied in each team: from large teams with as many as eight people, who each had clearly defined roles and responsibilities, to small leadership teams that acted as one homogenous group and thought of themselves as three heads of the same beast. The headteacher's level of involvement with the SLT varied at each school too: some headteachers wanted to meet daily and be involved with every decision, whereas others preferred to check in once a week and only hear the headlines. Regardless of the structure of the SLT, each member will be responsible for a different area, such as safeguarding, assessment, or health and safety. If you're new to the school, get a copy of the staffing structure as soon as you can – this will ensure that you know who is the correct person to approach with any issues. As a middle leader it is important that you have clear communication and maintain a strong working relationship with your SLT. Here are five tips that will help you do just that.

**1**  Remember, the SLT are there to support you.

In the same way that it is your responsibility to develop and support members of your team, your SLT have a duty to develop and support you. A good SLT should help you to develop your leadership skills through coaching, modelling or simply by setting a good example in their own practice. They should offer you CPD opportunities, including training and opportunities to deliver INSET, or encourage you to take on further responsibility. Be honest with them about the support you need – speak to them if you're struggling because they will be able to help.

**2**  Be honest.

As I said in Chapter 1, you aren't going to agree with every decision the SLT make – that's OK. If you find yourself at odds with what the SLT want to do, speak up. Keep it professional: be specific about what you don't agree with, explain why and be prepared to offer an alternative approach. For example, 'I have a few concerns about the proposed marking policy. I believe that it will create extra work for our staff, who are already stretched. I've done some research and I've found a few examples of other school marking policies that we could consider adapting.' What you say may not influence their final decision, but it's important to voice your opinions because it will be your job to implement new policies and initiatives within your team.

**3**  Be proactive.

Be proactive if there is something you want to implement in your subject or phase. Present your idea to the SLT and explain exactly what you want to do and why. There are two valuable reasons for doing this. Firstly, the SLT can offer useful feedback and advice on your idea. Secondly, your work will be noticed. Schools are busy places and it's important that your leadership team see that you are dealing with any problems or challenges within your department and are coming up with solutions and ideas. The relationship between middle leaders and the SLT shouldn't just consist of middle leaders bringing all their problems to the SLT for them to solve. It is the SLT's job to support you but offer them suggested solutions as often as you take them problems.

4   Share research.

Have you read something that you think the SLT should read? Email it on. Don't wait for a meeting to share it. I'm frequently sending my headteacher research and ideas with the message, 'I'm not suggesting we do this – but isn't it interesting?' She'll often come to me a few weeks later to discuss it and share her thoughts. Equally, I go to her to borrow education books from her office. Discussions about educational research are hugely beneficial – they make you question your practice, challenge your thinking and, ultimately, make you a better teacher.

5   Pass on praise.

Being a headteacher, deputy headteacher or assistant headteacher can be a thankless and sometimes lonely job. There is often very little appreciation for the work they do to ensure that the school is happy and effective, but there is plenty of vocal criticism whenever a mistake is made. When your SLT do something well, tell them. You don't have to praise specific actions; you can say something as simple as, 'I really enjoy working with you.' Praise from your own staff as a senior leader can mean more than praise from anybody else.

# The bridge

As a middle leader, maintaining the trust and respect of both the SLT and the rest of the staff is a delicate balancing act. Being 'in the middle', you can sometimes feel like you are a bridge between these two groups, with a foot in either camp. With good relationships, a strong leadership team and clear communication you should not feel that you have to take sides but, inevitably, there are occasions when your SLT will make a decision that the rest of the staff aren't happy with and this can present challenges. The stereotypical image of teachers moaning in the staffroom, I can happily report, is a load of rubbish (not least because teachers barely have time to get to the staffroom for longer than 20 minutes). In my experience, the staffroom has been a place of interesting discussion, support and plenty of laughter. However, there are times when teachers need to let off steam and there is every chance that you could find yourself sat around a table while your colleagues moan about a decision the SLT have made. In this situation you have three options – and with experience you'll learn to judge which is the right course of action for the situation you find yourself in.

1  Don't worry about it.

   Your colleagues need to know that they can moan without it getting back to the SLT. Let your colleagues get things off their chests and don't worry about it.

2  Pass on their concerns.

   You don't want to do this too often. If morale seems genuinely low or if your colleagues are raising legitimate concerns about an increase in workload then it is time to say something. Think carefully about who to speak to and how you package their concerns. Approach a member of SLT you have a good relationship with and avoid mentioning individual members of staff by name. You could say something vague such as, 'I was in the staffroom at lunchtime and I think there are a few concerns from the staff we need to address.'

3  Reassure your colleagues.

   If you can answer your colleagues' concerns and feel comfortable doing so, then use the informal setting of the staffroom to do this. Keep it casual but honest, e.g. 'I know what you mean, but at the same time I understand why they've taken this decision.' If you have similar concerns, then you can tell your colleagues that you will speak to the SLT about them – this will reassure them that the matter is being dealt with. Sometimes you'll find staff concerns aren't linked directly to new initiatives that have been introduced but to possible consequences that they fear haven't been considered, for example that a change in routine will have an impact on children's behaviour or a new monitoring process will impact on workload. Use this opportunity to discuss how these consequences could be avoided and reassure them that, if these consequences materialise, you will speak to the SLT if they don't feel comfortable doing so. Ultimately, you want to get to the position where you feel happy to do this, but it may take some time, particularly if you are new to a school.

# The governing body

The school hierarchy is more than just staff – a host of other influences have a say in how the school is run and the decisions that are made. Perhaps the most obvious is the governing body. The relationship between the governing body and the school is incredibly important. On matters such as safeguarding, the school site and the budget, it is the governors who have the final say. It is their role to act as a critical friend to the school and its leadership, holding them to account but also offering support and guidance where appropriate. According to the National Governance Association, the role of the governing body is to:

- Set the aims and objectives for the school and targets for meeting them.
- Set the policies for achieving those aims and objectives.
- Monitor and evaluate the school's progress towards achieving its aims and objectives.
- Challenge and support the headteacher. (National Governance Association, 2018)

### Reporting to governors
As a middle leader, you are contributing to the school's progress towards achieving its aims and objectives. Therefore, it will be your job to report the key headlines from your phase, subject or whole-school responsibility to governors on a termly basis. This can be done by writing a short paragraph to be included in the headteacher's termly report to the

governing body or by attending a governors' or committee meeting to report on the work you've been doing. If you're asked to contribute to the headteacher's report, remember to use the third person, a formal tone, and data to support your claims. Here's an example.

---

### KS2 English

Our school improvement target has been to develop staff's subject knowledge of grammar. This term our English leader, Rebecca Andrews, delivered three hours of INSET to the staff. The feedback we received from this training through staff questionnaires has been very positive: over 85 per cent of staff said the training was 'very useful' and 81 per cent said that it had already improved their practice. In addition to this training, Rebecca has been team teaching with teachers in Years 3 and 4 and has plans to do the same for Years 5 and 6 next term. Our most recent assessments show there has been a six per cent increase in the number of pupils meeting and exceeding National Expectations in spelling, punctuation and grammar. In writing 69 per cent of children are meeting or exceeding National Expectations, which is a seven per cent increase on last term.

---

If you attend a governors' meeting to report directly to them, be prepared to answer questions and have your data headlines and targets to hand so you can use them to support your answers.

## Link governors

It has become common practice for schools to assign governors to specific phases and subjects. If you find yourself in this position, try to make regular (monthly or half-termly) contact with your link governor and keep them up to date on the work you're doing. Invite them in for an informal visit to come and see lessons and talk to teachers – don't wait for governors' day. Remember, you are the expert: governors are not teachers or school leaders themselves. Some may have children in school, but others may not have set foot in a school since they were children. They are not qualified to comment on the quality of teaching or work they see in books. When you're inviting them in, they are coming to find out what a normal day is like at your school, not to make a judgement on your practice.

# Dealing with parents

There is one group of stakeholders I am yet to address and it is a group that you'll encounter far more regularly than governors – parents. It is interesting that the relationship between parents and their child's school can be so precarious because, ultimately, both parties want the same thing – for the child to be happy and successful. But relationships with parents require careful management. Parents need to know they are appreciated and listened to, but it also needs to be made clear that they do not run the school. If you've ever worked at a school that jumps through hoops to meet every parent's frivolous whim, you'll know the problems it can cause.

Before I get into the nitty-gritty of how to deal with difficult parents, it's important to remember that the parents are not one homogenous group, so you should not treat them as such. In fact, most parents are harmless: they drop their children off at school and just want to know that their child will be learning, happy and safe until they come home at the end of the day. Difficult parents are likely to be in the minority. The bad news is, as a middle leader, you'll be considered a port of call for parents who want to complain. The good news is, as a middle leader, there are plenty of people senior to you who can support you or even take over the management of the complaint when necessary.

Let's start with an example. You're on duty at the end of the day and an angry parent comes marching over to you. She tells you that her son is being bullied and that the class teacher knows about it but is refusing to do anything about it. The nature of the complaint may vary, but my advice for dealing with parent complaints does not. Here are four key tips:

1   Get indoors.

    If possible, invite the parent indoors to discuss the issue further. This means that you avoid the gaze of other parents on the playground and it stops other people from 'helpfully' getting involved. If the parent refuses to go inside, don't panic – you'll just need to stay calm and manage the situation.

2   Stay calm.

    It's vital that you stay in control of the situation and that means keeping calm. Let the parent finish their rant and listen – you could make notes so that you don't forget any of the details. Don't feel as though you have to resolve the complaint there and then. Explain to the parent that you will follow up the complaint with the people involved. That is all they need to know.

**3**  Maintain a united front and don't criticise other members of staff.

No matter what you think about the member of staff who the parent is complaining about, you absolutely must not criticise that member of staff. As a middle leader you have a responsibility to look after the staff in your team. Get the parent to write down the complaint (or make notes as they talk) and promise to follow it up with the teacher in question. Follow it up as soon as you can with the member of staff concerned, in private.

**4**  If you need to, pass it on.

There are a number of people in your school who are more senior to you so use them. Go to them for advice and, if you really feel out of your depth, ask if they can take over managing the complaint or at least help you deal with it. Don't struggle alone.

Every school receives complaints from parents. A parent making a complaint in the playground is not something that other parents will remember. What will stay with them is how the complaint was dealt with. So, stay calm and try to keep the conversation adult-to-adult if possible (see Chapter 4).

## Parent workshops

Parent workshops are a fantastic way to strengthen the relationship between staff and parents because they help parents understand how to support their child with their education. They are also important for making sure the parents and the school are on the same page. How many times have you had a parent say, 'I want to help with his maths homework, but I don't know which methods you're teaching. I only know what I did when I was at school'? Workshops can smooth out these issues and are a prime opportunity to explain your curriculum and the reasoning behind it.

Planning a parent workshop is very similar to planning an INSET (see Chapter 8): be evidence based, start with why and make the objective of the talk clear. However, there is one crucial difference: when you are talking to the parents, you are the expert. Unlike in a staff INSET, you can't rely on the parents having their own prior knowledge to bring to the training. They are there because they want to learn from you. You can present the parents with questions to consider and offer prompts for group discussions, but most of the parent workshop will be you talking and answering questions. Here's my advice:

1  Keep it simple, avoiding educational jargon and acronyms.

2  Provide a handout that summarises the talk for parents to take home with them. They may want it to refer to in the future.

3  Avoid using examples of specific classes and year groups. Even something as innocent as, 'They do this very well in Year 5' may be interpreted as it not being done very well in all other year groups.

4  Try to repeat the workshop two or three times a term to make it as convenient as possible for parents to attend. For example, you could run a session before school, a session straight after the morning drop-off and a session after school. Consider running the workshop on an evening when the parents are already in school, for example parents' evening. This way, class teachers can direct parents over to the workshop during their meeting with them. 'If you would like more advice on how you can support Fred with his maths at home then I know that our maths leader is running a workshop in the hall in about half an hour. It might be worth dropping in.'

Here is a word of warning: the parents who attend parent workshops are likely to be the ones who are already reading with their children, helping with homework and making sure they have their homework, book bag or clean PE kit. Unfortunately, the parents who really need your support may not be there, so make sure you find a way to get this information out to them too by email or putting it on the school website.

Good relationships are at the heart of running any school and maintaining them should be a priority. Good relationships are never complete – circumstances can change and trust can be eroded far more quickly than it can be earned – so they require constant work. Maintaining good relationships at the same time as holding your team to account through regular monitoring can be challenging, but there is no reason why the two should be mutually exclusive. Luckily for you this is what Chapter 6 is all about.

# Chapter 6
# Monitoring

A question you're likely to be asked by Ofsted or any other interested visitors is: 'How do you know what is happening in classrooms on a day-to-day basis?' An Ofsted inspector once told my husband, 'When I visit a school I'm not interested in the bells and whistles; I want to know what is happening on a grey Tuesday morning in February.' The point she was making was that it's the day-to-day teaching and learning that matters. So, how can you be sure that the carefully thought-out policy you wrote in Chapter 3 is actually being followed? And, most importantly, how do you find all of this out without eroding trust within your team or damaging the positive relationships you've worked so hard to build? The answer is monitoring.

For pupils, the word 'monitor' has positive connotations. It means having responsibility; it means you're trusted by your teacher; and it might even mean you get to wear a badge. Young children will eagerly jostle to take on all number of banal, repetitive tasks in the name of being a 'monitor': from watering plants and handing out fruit to tidying the teacher's desk. For staff the term 'monitor' means lesson observations, book looks, learning walks, progress meetings and submitting spreadsheet after spreadsheet of data for scrutiny. Whether monitoring is a positive or negative experience depends on how it is managed. The complaints about monitoring are almost always regarding how often it happens, how much it disrupts class routine and whether the process is considered fair.

## When do you carry out monitoring?

How often monitoring occurs depends entirely on the school. Some schools have an open-door policy in which all staff are encouraged to observe one another on a regular basis. Other schools set aside a specific week or fortnight each term for observations and monitoring. Whatever the policy is at your school, I would advocate a mix of formal observations and regular drop-ins, learning walks or book looks.

Try to minimise the disruption. For example, if you want to take a set of pupils' books for scrutiny, try to schedule this for a time when the pupils won't need them. Whilst it may be best for you to take books home for the weekend to have an in-depth look, you should always check that the teacher wasn't planning to take them home to mark first.

## How do you carry out monitoring?

The most common methods used to monitor teaching and learning are observing lessons, speaking to children, looking at work in books and analysing the data. Each of these methods gives us just one piece of the puzzle; it's not until you look at all four areas together that you get the whole picture of what's going on in the classroom (we'll go into this in more detail at the end of the chapter). It's therefore important that you use all of these methods in your monitoring, so let's look at each in turn. First up, observations.

## Observations

Observing other teachers is one of the privileges of being a middle leader. I love spending time in other people's classrooms – it's an excellent opportunity to develop your own practice because you always learn something new from watching others teach. For your first observation it is likely that you'll have a second member of staff with you because it's useful to have someone to bounce ideas off and discuss the lesson with. Remember to keep in mind that a once-a-term lesson observation is a snapshot – all it really tells you is how well prepared the teacher was for that observation.

In 2013 the Sutton Trust published research on classroom monitoring and found that, 'Even when conducted by well-trained, independent evaluators, classroom observations are the least predictive method of assessing teacher effectiveness.' (Murphy, 2013) That's not to say they aren't worthwhile. Any opportunity that enables feedback for colleagues is useful and, besides, it's also an opportunity to talk to pupils and look at their work.

How often you will conduct observations will probably be decided by the SLT. To get a real picture of what's happening, regular and low-key drop-ins are often more useful than high-stakes formal observations. In my first year as a super-keen NQT, I used to go over the top for observations. The night (and week) before would be spent creating colourful, laminated resources and all-singing, all-dancing slides (literally in some cases), and writing a lesson plan that read like a short story. I treated observations like a performance: the resources were my props; my plan was my script; and I would easily spend up to eight hours preparing for the one lesson that was going to be observed. Generally, the observations would go well – the member of staff observing would feel satisfied that I knew what I was doing – and the day would continue. The lessons I taught after the observation lesson, however, were always appalling. Seriously terrible. I would have spent so much time preparing for the observation that I wouldn't have left myself time to think about the rest of the day or the week. My poor class would start the day with an outstanding lesson, but then they wouldn't learn anything else for the rest of the day. The member of staff who had observed my stage-managed performance left with a false impression about my abilities as a teacher. It was a very easy game to play and benefited no one.

Thankfully, things have moved on in the last eight years and teachers' performance is no longer based on once-a-term observations. It's widely accepted that 'little and often' is more useful for everyone than one high-stakes observation. As a middle leader, I try to pop into classes on a weekly basis and these drop-ins are sometimes just for ten minutes.

Drop-ins should not be used to catch members of staff out. Make them positive experiences by being openly enthusiastic about the lesson you've walked in on. Find the class teacher at the end of the day to say,

'It was great to see X happening in your classroom when I popped in earlier – well done!'

## What to look for

When conducting an observation always ask yourself, 'Are the children learning? Does the teacher have the subject knowledge and the skills needed to help children make progress? Are the relationships between pupils and staff in the classroom respectful, positive and conducive to learning?' Ultimately, this is what you are assessing. It's important that you don't bring your own biases about teaching into observations. You may have a preferred teaching style or method but, as long as the children are learning (and the teaching isn't in some way undermining or ignoring the school policy), then keep an open mind. It's too easy to approach observations with a mental tick list, but this can be restrictive.

In the first few years of my career I used to have a long tick list in my head. It was based on advice I'd been given and, in some cases, actual checklists that I'd been judged on in the past. It looked something like this:

| The over-worked primary school lesson observation proforma | |
| --- | --- |
| Teacher _____ Subject _____ | |
| Date _____ Grade ____ (1 Outstanding, 2 Good, 3 Satisfactory, 4 Inadequate) | |
| Descriptors | Comments |
| ✓ The teacher has shared the learning objective and success criteria.<br>✓ The objective is appropriate for the year group.<br>✓ Teacher talk minimised to less than 15 per cent of the lesson.<br>✓ Questioning is differentiated.<br>✓ Work is differentiated to support the varying needs of the class.<br>✓ Different learning styles are catered for.<br>✓ Tables are clear and tidy. | |

| |
|---|
| ✓ Work from the previous lesson is marked.<br>✓ Resources are clearly labelled.<br>✓ Displays are relevant, eye-catching and interactive.<br>✓ Teacher works with a guided group.<br>✓ Teacher uses lolly stick-style system for random questioning.<br>✓ Pupils encouraged to work with a talk partner.<br>✓ The lesson ends with a plenary.<br>✓ The teacher returns to the learning objective and the success criteria.<br>✓ All pupils have made accelerated progress during the lesson.<br>✓ Support staff are sat with a guided group.<br>✓ Teachers use a range of questions (Bloom's).<br>✓ All pupils met the learning objective.<br>✓ Pupil targets are up to date.<br>✓ Resources are on the table at the start of the lesson. | |

A few years ago, I observed a Year 6 history lesson that forced me to reflect on the checklist approach. It was a lesson about the causes of the Second World War. Although the objective and success criteria were not explicitly referred to or written down, what the pupils were learning about in the lesson was very clear. There was plenty of teacher talk; there was no guided group work (which is something I would have baulked at back in the day); the classroom was cluttered; and the displays were slightly shabby and clearly hadn't been updated for a while. The pupils listened in near silence while the teacher spoke; they asked interesting questions and occasionally discussed ideas with their partner. The atmosphere was quiet and purposeful and by the end of the lesson the whole class could explain the causes of the Second World War. Despite the fact that there were no laminated cards being passed around and discussed, no group work, no singing or dancing, the children learnt everything the teacher intended for them to learn. I graded the lesson 'Outstanding'. (This was back in the days when we still graded lessons).

Observing teaching means putting aside any preconceptions you have of the teacher and assessing what's going on in front of you. When I fed back to the member of staff afterwards I said, 'Based on the amount of learning that happened in that lesson, no one could say it was anything less than "Outstanding". However, if Ofsted turn up, I would stick an objective on the board as it's school policy.' Ofsted themselves have actually said time and time again that they have no preferred teaching style and so, as middle leaders, we should not be pushing teachers into teaching a certain way if their own methods and approach are proving to be successful and they are following the school policy.

All a tick list of criteria can tell you is what the person who wrote it believes 'Outstanding' teaching should look like. I've seen lessons that were all teacher talk and lessons that I wouldn't have been able to tick off half the above criteria for but that were still 'Outstanding' because of the amount the children learnt. It is the learning that matters. Tidy, interactive displays and an organised classroom look good and are perhaps a reflection of the class teacher's organisation skills, but they don't tell you how good that teacher is at teaching. If you think the classroom is so messy and unorganised that it's preventing the children from learning, then take up your concerns with the teacher. If not and the pupils know where everything they need is and all the evidence suggests that they're making good progress, then a messy desk does not signal a bad teacher.

So, abandon the checklist and just look for learning and subject knowledge. If the idea of walking in to observe a lesson with a blank sheet of paper, or even no paper at all, feels slightly overwhelming, divide your sheet into two simple columns: 'Strengths' and 'Areas for development'.

## Get involved while you're observing

Don't just sit at the back and watch. There is nothing more off-putting than a po-faced member of management sat at the back of the room, scribbling away on a clipboard for an hour. During the lesson, talk to the children, move around the tables and interact with the class teacher when possible and without interrupting the lesson.

Remember: you're looking for the learning. How do you find out if the children are learning? By talking to them. Simply asking, 'What are you learning about today?' is a good starting point. During the observation take time to listen in to the children's conversations without interrupting them as this will give you an insight into their understanding. Look at their books – is this lesson building on previous learning or consolidating? We've become obsessed in recent years with 'new learning', but lessons that consolidate learning are vital for building in-depth understanding. What's more important is whether the lesson is challenging both the most and the least able pupils.

At the end of the observation, whether it's been ten minutes or an hour, quietly thank the class teacher and the class and say goodbye.

## Feedback

Giving useful feedback is a real skill and it took me a good few months to really master it. Remember: you don't need to grade the lesson. Ofsted no longer grade individual lessons and state that they do 'not expect schools to use the Ofsted evaluation schedule to grade teaching or individual lessons.' (Ofsted, 2018) This makes giving feedback easier because it becomes a discussion between two colleagues about best practice rather than one colleague grading the other.

There are four basic steps to delivering lesson feedback:

1 Start with the positives.

2 Identify one or two specific areas that could be developed or improved.

3 Give a practical example of *how* they could improve those areas (this step is very important).

4 Thank the teacher and say how much you enjoyed being in their class.

That's the basic structure, but I promised I would provide practical advice that you could take into school with you – so, here's how the conversation could go:

| 1. Start with the positives. | 'Hi Emma. Thanks for having me in your lesson today. I know it's always a bit nerve-wracking being observed – we've all been through it. I love observing because it always gives me ideas to take back to my own class. Anyway, your lesson. I thought it was great. The pupils could all clearly identify the different types of rock by the end and the pupils I spoke to could explain how different types of rock are formed. Your subject knowledge is excellent: you provided pupils with in-depth explanations about rock formation and introduced them to the technical vocabulary. Your behaviour management was a real strength: you had the whole class's attention and kept on top of the low-level disruption that we know can sometimes be an issue in that class.' |
|---|---|
| 2. Identify one or two specific areas that could be developed or improved. | 'As far as areas to develop, there are a couple of small things to think about. Pupils like Mohammed and Sara could really have done with some more explicit modelling of the task. I noticed they weren't quite sure how to complete the activity once they went back to their tables. Next time consider modelling the task for the whole class before sending them to their seats.' |
| 3. Give a practical example of *how* they could improve those areas. | 'And there was one girl, Rebecca? She finished the task quite quickly and it would have been good to have something ready for her to move on to. For example, it could have been asking her to write an explanation of how igneous rocks are formed using the technical vocabulary that you'd introduced throughout the lesson. Does that make sense?' |
| 4. Thank the teacher and say how much you enjoyed being in their class. | 'Thanks again for having me in, Emma – it was a real pleasure to be part of that lesson.' |

By keeping the feedback specific and by giving an example, the teacher can act on the feedback almost immediately. There are times when you will observe a lesson that has not gone well. Giving feedback in these situations isn't easy. Turn to Chapter 7, 'Difficult conversations', for advice on how to do this.

# Talking to pupils

In 2008 I was part of a team of ICT middle leaders in a large primary school in North London. We conducted pupil interviews as part of a bi-annual audit and I was responsible for interviewing Year 6. I asked a bright Year 6 pupil, 'What could we do to make your computing lessons *even* better?' He responded, 'Well, the thing is, Mrs Paramour, I'm a Mac user and here we only have PCs – it's a bit of a problem for me.' I'm using this anecdote to highlight the flaw in pupil interviews – children are not teachers so they cannot accurately reflect on class needs and make viable suggestions for improvements, but that's not to say you shouldn't consult them as part of your monitoring. As with all methods of monitoring, pupil surveys aren't perfect and shouldn't be used in isolation. However, if they are clearly structured with age-appropriate questions, they can be a useful way of building up another part of the picture of what's going on in the classroom.

## How to conduct pupil interviews

First, choose a random sample of pupils. As tempting as it is to take the three most articulate and enthusiastic pupils from each class, you need a mixed sample in order to be representative. A simple announcement in the weekly staff meeting will do it: 'Could all class teachers send the first, 11th, and 23rd pupil from the register to my classroom at 2:15pm on Wednesday? I'd like to ask them some questions about their computing lessons.'

Decide if you want to give pupils a questionnaire to complete themselves or if you're going to ask them questions verbally and note their responses. It might be helpful to use a voice recorder to record some of their answers if you're going to be feeding back to staff later. In the box below are some examples of questions you could use – I wrote these when I was English middle leader, but they can be easily adapted for your subject or phase.

---

### Pupil interview questions

What have you been learning about in English this term?

What's the most interesting thing you've learnt in English?

How often do you read at school?

When do you read at home?

Tell me about the best English lesson you've had this year – what did you learn?

How do you know what to do to improve your work?

What are your targets?

Do you enjoy your English lessons? Why? Why not?

What could the school do to make English lessons *even* better?

What do you do if you find you're stuck in a lesson?

---

Talking to pupils gives us a unique insight into how they perceive their time in school. A small word of warning: memories are easily manipulated, and children may give the answers they think you want to hear rather than tell you a truth that might upset or disappoint you. For example, it's quite common for children to try to impress their teachers by claiming they find all the work 'really easy', which is why you should also check their books. Younger children, in particular, have relatively short memories so don't be too alarmed if you hear something like, 'We NEVER do geography in Year 1', because it could just mean they that haven't had a geography lesson for a couple of weeks.

An alternative to the pupil interview is to follow a child for a day. Choose a child to track all day: sit next to them in lessons, eat lunch with them and even spend time with them out on the playground. This is particularly useful if you are a phase leader because it will give you a picture of what the offer is to children in your phase on a daily basis. You may want to repeat this with a child in every year group in your phase. The conversations you'll have over the course of the day will be invaluable and tell you a lot about what happens each day in your phase.

# Book scrutiny

Now that we've moved away from judging teachers' effectiveness on the basis of one-off lesson observations, more weight is given to work evidenced in children's books. Scrutiny can be done in a number of different ways. I've always found it more effective to go through books with the class teacher because it makes the process a dialogue rather than a judgement. As with observations, there is a difference between informal and formal book scrutiny. Informal scrutiny can be done when you're popping into lessons or on a learning walk – have a quick flick through the children's books and ask them some questions about their work. Formal book scrutiny tends to be more in-depth and you are often required to keep a record of the findings. How many books you look at is up to you, but the more you look at, the more you'll have an idea of what is typical for the class. As a class teacher there is nothing more frustrating than a middle or senior leader picking up two or three books and making a judgement. I'd argue you need at least a third of the class's work to get the real picture. So, *what* are you looking for when you look in children's books?

1 Marking and feedback

   Is there evidence of feedback? Does the feedback follow the school's policy? Furthermore, is there evidence that the teacher's marking has had an impact on the pupil's work? If every lesson Sam is asked to 'add capital letters and full stops' to his sentences and he still isn't doing so, it might be time to try a different approach.

2 Presentation

   This one is straightforward enough: are the children being asked to follow the school's presentation policy? Is there evidence that presentation has improved over the course of the year? Does it look as though the teacher is enforcing the handwriting policy (if your school has one)?

3 Progress

   Have the children learnt anything this year? Look at the work from the beginning of the year and compare it with the most recent pieces.

**4**   Curriculum coverage

This is particularly relevant for subject leaders. Is the National Curriculum for that year group being covered? Are the objectives appropriate and what areas of the curriculum do they need to cover by the end of the year?

## Things to remember when scrutinising books

Be realistic. As we've already discussed, middle leaders are in the unique position of having management responsibilities and being full-time class teachers. This means you understand better than anyone the pressures of keeping on top of marking and know that if the teacher hasn't marked the last piece of work (or even the last three) it doesn't mean that the teacher is failing or not following the school's marking policy. It could just be a case of having a conversation with that member of staff and seeing if there's a reason they're struggling to keep on top of everything. If in doubt, speak to the teacher.

'Why is there no work in Joshua's book for THREE CONSECUTIVE DAYS?' was the feedback I once received after a book look. Generally, my books were always up to date and well-presented, especially once I became a middle leader, because it was important to me that I led by example. The reason there was no work in Joshua's book for 'THREE CONSECUTIVE DAYS' was because Joshua had been off school sick the previous week. If you see something that doesn't look quite right in a book, go and speak to the class teacher because there's probably a perfectly reasonable explanation. It is likely that the book is the exception not the rule.

# Data

Whatever your view on data, it is part of school life and, as a middle leader, it will be your job to collect and analyse it. According to a report from the Sutton Trust, 'Gains in pupil test scores are the best available metric to measure teacher performance.' (Murphy, 2013) In my experience, this is broadly true: if there are no additional barriers to learning (such as SEN), a pupil who is receiving consistently good teaching will score better on a test at the end of the school year than they do in September. Test scores are the only form of quantitative data we have for judging pupil and teacher performance and we use it to justify and condemn all manner of things in primary education. Results and test scores are important but, as with pupil interviews and lesson observations, it is important to view them as part of the bigger picture.

## How to collect data

How often you collect assessment data will be decided by your SLT, but in most schools it's once a term. Any more frequently than that and it can start to feel a bit like you're testing more than you're teaching. Just to be clear, I'm talking about formal, summative assessment data, not in-class quizzes and other forms of formative assessment. For the most accurate data, try to ensure that it is the same format of test being administered: there's little to be gained from comparing NFER test results with OCR so choose the tests you want and stick with them for the year.

## Data definitions

Before we start asking questions about the data it's worth knowing the following definitions:

**Attainment:** The grade, score or level.

**Progress:** How much pupils' attainment has increased since the beginning of the year or key stage.

**Achievement:** An Ofsted judgement that takes into account both attainment and progress.

**National Expectations:** The government's expectations of what pupils should attain nationally.

## Questions to ask about data

Once you've got the raw score back from the teachers, it's likely you'll be faced with a spreadsheet of numbers. Don't panic. The first thing to do is order the pupils from the highest attaining to the lowest attaining and have a look at the pupils at the bottom of your list. Start by focusing on their attainment. Consider the following questions:

- Are these pupils from a particular group, e.g. SEN, EAL, ethnic minorities, looked after children?

- Has the class teacher identified these pupils as those in need of further support? (I guarantee you they have – teachers don't need test scores to tell them which pupils are falling behind.)

- What are the reasons these pupils aren't reaching National Expectations?

- What could be done to support these pupils?

- How does the attainment reached at the end of each key stage compare with the national average?

- Has attainment of one particular group or subject improved or dropped significantly? If so, why? What strategies are in place to sustain and share good practice and bring about further improvements?

- Are some individuals and groups of pupils doing better than others? If so, why might this be?

## Progress

Progress is more important than attainment. You work out the progress by comparing the attainment from the previous term to the most recent attainment. Then consider the following questions:

- Are pupils making better- or worse-than-expected rates of progress each year?

- Compare groups (e.g. looked after children, boys, girls, ethnic groups, each group of SEN pupils, gifted and talented pupils). Are some individuals and groups of pupils and some subjects making better progress than others?

- What might be the reasons for some pupils making slower progress than others? If so, why? What strategies are in place to sustain and share good practice and bring about improvements?

It can be easy to get bogged down with data – we focus on it far too much in primary schools and we use it in ways that would make a statistician weep. Using data to talk about a sample size of 60 children is farcical so try to treat the data for what it is: another way of working out what your pupils need.

# Reflect on your monitoring

After a round of monitoring it's important to reflect on your findings. Gather together your notes from your observations and book scrutiny, the pupil survey responses and your data analysis, and ask yourself: does the evidence match up? This is often referred to as triangulation: each area of monitoring is like the corner of a triangle and the evidence links the three corners up. It's like the final scene of a murder mystery: you sit down and check that all your evidence points to the same conclusion. Questions to consider are:

- Does the data reflect the quality of teaching you've seen in your observations?

- Does the quality of work match what the data says? For example, if a child is said to be 'working at greater depth', is there evidence of this in their books?

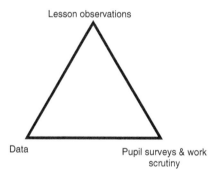

Figure: Triangulation

If the answer to any of these questions is 'no', don't worry, just make a note of it and keep an eye on it in the future. If the issue is poor data from a teacher that is by all other suggestions good, then just follow it up with the class teacher. It is standard practice for schools to have termly progress meetings to discuss how all the pupils are getting on and this would be a good opportunity to ask any questions you have. Just something like, 'How's Oliver getting on? The work in his books is good but his scores are quite low. Is there anything we need to put in place for him? How is he in lessons?' Once again, this makes the process a dialogue rather than something that is being done to catch teachers out or create more stress for them.

Once you've looked at the evidence and joined the corners of the triangle, take some time to reflect on how your department is going as a whole by asking yourself the following questions:

- What's going well in your department? (We often forget to celebrate the positives and focus entirely on the weaknesses. Make a list of everything that is going well in your department and share it with your team.)

- What surprised you? What did you find out about your department that you didn't know before? It could be, 'X teacher is fantastic at giving clear, concise explanations' or, 'Y's behaviour management is spot on.' (Remember to go and tell those teachers you were impressed!)

- Which areas need to be developed? This could be an area from your action plan that you are yet to implement or something more general that you've identified from your monitoring, e.g. transitions between lessons need to be smoother or pupils need more opportunities for extended writing. Choose just one or two things to work on.

- Do any of your team members need some extra support? Sadly, in some schools, 'support' has become a euphemism for pushing a teacher out, or bombarding them with unnecessary observations and being overly critical until they decide to leave, but that shouldn't be how it is. If you've noticed that someone in your team is struggling, now is the time to go and have a conversation with them to find out if there is anything they need your help with, whether that's planning lessons or team teaching. For more advice about what to do if a member of staff is really struggling, head to the next chapter, 'Difficult conversations'. In fact, let's go there now.

# Chapter 7
# Difficult conversations

*Jessica is late for work every morning. School starts at 8:50am and she can often be seen walking in with the children. She works in Year 5 and the rest of the Year 5 team are getting frustrated as she gets in too late to set up properly for the day, so throughout the morning children from her class appear at their door asking to borrow equipment and resources. One of her parallel teachers comes to you and asks you to speak to her. He explains that the team have spoken to her about it, but it's not made any difference.*

Whilst I hope you won't need to use this chapter too often, difficult conversations are part of leadership. We've all worked with someone who is not pulling their weight and moaned with our colleagues that their line manager has not spoken to them about it. In the scenario above, your team have tried to solve the problem themselves and have come to you for support. For their team to work effectively, they need you, as the phase leader, to have a conversation with Jessica about her punctuality. If you avoid having the difficult conversation, you will let your team down and undersell yourself as a leader. You send out the message that Jessica's behaviour is acceptable and, as Susan Scott (2011) has pointed out, 'as a leader, you get what you tolerate'. Most importantly, by not having the conversation, you don't give Jessica the chance to improve her behaviour.

You should know that I am one of the least confrontational people you'll ever meet. At the beginning of my career I would always choose to do something myself over having to ask someone else to do it and risk upsetting them. In 2011 I went on holiday to New York and was served a slice of cheesecake that had mould growing on it. I had to be persuaded by my friend to ask them to swap it for a fresh piece. That's how difficult I found it to confront people. For me, confronting somebody meant I was being rude, unhelpful or unreasonable.

Having difficult conversations was something I had to work at. It did not come naturally to me at all and, even after years of practice, I still find it hard. If you're anything like me and can't imagine having to tell someone that their lesson didn't go well or that they need to mark their books more regularly, then I hope this chapter will help because handling these conversations is a vital part of being an effective leader. You may never find these kinds of conversations easy, but there are things you can do to make them easier. I am now able to confidently navigate difficult conversations at work (although I still hate complaining in restaurants).

# Difficult conversations: general guidance

Before we consider the specifics of the conversation you might have with Jessica, here is some general guidance to keep in mind if you have to have a difficult conversation with someone in your team.

### Ask for advice
There is no shame in going to another member of staff to ask for advice – just make sure it is a member of staff senior to you, or even a more experienced middle leader. You will not be the first person who has had to have this sort of conversation. Draw on the expertise of the people around you. There's no reason for you to face these situations on your own.

### Plan and practise the conversation
You need to act quickly once the issue has been raised. The longer you sit on it, the more of a big deal the conversation will become. Decide when and where to have the conversation. If possible, I would always choose to have the conversation in that person's classroom, where they feel more comfortable. Think about where are you going to sit in the classroom. As tempting as it can be to stay standing so you can walk straight out, it

can look as though you're not there to listen to the teacher if you stay on your feet. Ideally, have the conversation at the end of the school day so the teacher can go straight home afterwards and process the discussion you've had. If you have the conversation before school, the teacher has to teach all day with the conversation buzzing around their head.

Once you've sorted out the logistics, start planning what you're going to say. Practise your opening line to avoid waffling, so in the example of the scenario above it could be something like this: 'Hi Jessica, I just wanted to have a quick chat with you about your punctuality. A few people have noticed that you're getting in with the children in the morning, which doesn't leave you much time to get ready for your lessons. Is there something making you late?'

After your opening line, it's important to listen to the person you're talking to and respond to them. You won't be able to script the entire conversation, but you should plan your key points. For example, in the conversation with Jessica you would want to make sure you are clear about the following things:

- Directed time is from 8:30am, so all staff are expected to be on site from that time.

- The reason for this is to give time for year group teams to catch up with each other and talk through the day and to discuss plans with learning support assistants.

- Is there anything preventing Jessica from getting to school at 8:30am? If so, what could you do to help?

- Tell Jessica you'll pop back in next week to see how she's been getting on.

## Power posing

In 2012, social psychologist Amy Cuddy gave a TED Talk called 'Your body language may shape who you are'. It's worth a watch. She explains that there are postures we make when we are feeling confident or powerful like putting our hands on our hips and standing with our shoulders back. Her research has found that just striking those poses can increase your confidence (Cuddy, 2012). So, as silly as you may feel, stand with your hands on your hips as it can give you the confidence to get through the conversation. It was a technique famously deployed by the Conservative Party at their conference in 2015 – you can find photographs of George Osborne and Theresa May in some bizarre-looking stances. Whether or not power poses actually make a difference is still up for debate. Critics of the theory say the original experiment was flawed and had a sample size of 42, which makes it statistically irrelevant. However, in 2016 University College London published a study supporting the idea (Newman et al., 2016). You'll just have to see if it works for you, but I believe there is something to be said for faking it until you make it.

## Be objective

This isn't a personal attack – you're reminding a member of staff of their professional responsibilities to their team and their class. It doesn't come with judgement. In the context of this scenario, it's probably best to avoid saying to Jessica, 'Your team have asked me to speak to you.' This could destroy the trust between Jessica and her colleagues and could give the impression that people have been talking about her behind her back or that you are on their side. As the senior person in this conversation it is your responsibility to make sure it stays adult-to-adult (see Chapter 4).

## Listen more than you talk

Not that you would, but try to avoid sounding like you're delivering a script, no matter how much you've rehearsed the conversation beforehand. Go in to the conversation prepared to listen to what the other person has to say. There could be a very legitimate reason as to why Jessica has been late so often recently, so avoid going into the situation with your mind already made up and be ready to give her the benefit of the doubt. Showing that you're listening sends out the message that you value Jessica and are genuinely interested in helping her. No matter how tempting it may be, try to avoid interrupting or jumping in. Let Jessica speak until she's said everything she needs before responding.

## Be human but remain in control of your emotions

You can't control how the other member of staff will react, but you can control your own response. Jessica might get upset or angry and she might cry or shout. It's important you stay calm and don't get emotional but that doesn't mean you can't behave with compassion: 'I'm sorry you're upset, Jessica. Is there anything I can do to help?'

## Follow up

Research has found that, following a difficult conversation, more than 75 per cent of leaders felt satisfied with the outcome but only 46 per cent of staff confronted felt the same (Jones, 2016). Make sure you end the conversation by setting a time to follow up. Don't leave it too long – a week is long enough to have seen some change but not too long that the conversation will have faded from memory. The follow-up is also your opportunity to work on your relationship with that member of staff and build bridges. For example, if Jessica has been getting in on time consistently since you spoke to her, use the follow-up as a chance to praise her: 'Thanks for taking that on board, Jessica. It's made such a difference to your team and I can see how much more focused your class are when I pop in during morning lessons.'

Don't forget to follow up with the rest of Jessica's team too. There's no need to go into the specifics of the conversation but it's important that they know you took their concerns seriously and dealt with them.

Those are the basic steps. Now let's try applying them to some situations you might face as a middle leader.

# Scenarios

All of the scenarios described below I've encountered at some stage in my career. Some I dealt with effectively, but others I didn't and have since learnt from my mistakes. You won't get it right every time but that's OK as long as you can learn from where you went wrong. Let's start with the most common scenario you're likely to face: the bad lesson.

## Scenario 1: the bad lesson

You've observed a lesson and it hasn't gone very well. The first thing to establish is whether you've observed a great teacher who just had a bad lesson or if it's a teacher who is genuinely struggling. There is a big difference. A good teacher who's had a bad lesson will probably tell you the lesson didn't go well and they will probably be able to explain what went wrong and how they'd improve on it next time. A common pitfall in observations is that people try to put on an all-singing, all-dancing performance that is drastically different to their normal day and the class, not recognising it as their normal routine, act up as a result. I saw one great teacher attempt a carousel of activities with her class for the first time during an observation. The children weren't used to it so the transition between tables took most of the lesson and they learnt nothing. She took a risk and it didn't work. It doesn't mean she's a bad teacher – it was just a lesson that didn't go well.

In Chapter 6 we went over the basic structure for delivering feedback after a lesson observation:

1  Start with the positives.

2  Identify one or two specific areas that could be developed or improved.

3  Give a practical example of *how* they could improve those areas (this step is very important).

4  Thank the teacher and say how much you enjoyed being in their class.

When feeding back on a lesson that hasn't gone well, you can still use this structure, but you need to add an additional step in between steps three and four:

1  Start with the positives. No matter how bad the lesson was you can always find a positive, whether it's a comment on the learning environment, the relationships in the classroom or the resources.

2  Identify one or two specific areas that could be developed or improved. If there are several, pick the two most crucial areas to develop to avoid overwhelming the teacher.

3  Give a practical example of *how* the teacher could improve those areas and provide as much support as you can to help with this. In the conversation below the middle leader prints out some resources for the teacher that will help him

improve his teaching. If you can, come to the feedback session prepared.

**4** Agree a time in the next couple of weeks for you to go and observe the teacher again.

**5** Thank the teacher and say how much you enjoyed being in their class.

Not having to give a grade will make this easier – it makes it more of a professional dialogue and you can keep the conversation positive and constructive. All you're doing is setting a few targets that will enable the teacher to improve. That teacher doesn't walk away feeling labelled as 'Inadequate' or 'Requires Improvement'. Here's how the conversation could go.

| 1. Start with the positives. | 'Hi Mike. Thanks for having me in your lesson today. I know it's always a bit nerve-wracking being observed – we've all been through it. I love observing other people teach. It's a real privilege and I always learn something from it. What was really clear throughout the lesson, Mike, is that you've built up an excellent relationship with that class. They respond well to you and you're consistent with your behaviour management, which is evident from their behaviour.' |
|---|---|
| 2. Identify one or two specific areas that could be developed or improved. | 'As far as areas to develop, there are a few things I'd like you to think about. Firstly, I think I would have expected more challenge for Year 5. The lesson was about using adjectives to describe nouns, which is actually a KS1 objective. I think the work wasn't pitched correctly and there wasn't really the opportunity to extend them once they'd completed that task, which is why they all finished so quickly. The new grammar curriculum is particularly challenging so it's important your own subject knowledge is up to date – you need to be two steps ahead of your class.' |

| 3. Give a practical example of *how* they could improve those areas. | 'I've printed off the English programme of study for Year 5 so that you can see the sort of things that we'd expect to see being taught, for example converting nouns and adjectives into verbs by adding a suffix. Have you seen this programme of study before? It's quite useful for when you're planning. With regards to improving your subject knowledge, David Crystal has written a brilliant guide called *Rediscover Grammar*, which I can recommend if you feel that's one of your weaker areas.\* I used it to get myself up to date when the new curriculum came out because the content included things I hadn't used since I was in school myself.' |
|---|---|
| 4. Agree a time in the next couple of weeks for you to go and observe the teacher again. | 'I really don't want you to feel worried about this, Mike. It's very easily sorted. I'm going to ask Kate, as English leader, to pop into your PPA and help with your planning for the next few weeks. Is there a good time for me to come back and watch another lesson in the next couple of weeks? What about Tuesday 8th?' |
| 5. Thank the teacher and say how much you enjoyed being in their class. | 'Thanks again for having me in, Mike. I'm looking forward to seeing you teach again in a couple of weeks.' |

\*Incidentally, this really IS a brilliant book and it's my strongly held belief that every teacher should have a copy in their classroom. David Crystal is the grammar king – or he would be if that were an actual thing.

By following those steps Mike has a really clear idea of what he needs to do to improve. You haven't made him feel as though he is a bad teacher – you've shown empathy for how difficult it is keeping your subject knowledge up to date and have offered him practical solutions.

## Scenario 2: the luddite

This scenario is surprisingly common. A teacher in your team never checks his emails and is missing meetings and information. Deal with it early on. Make it clear to your team at the beginning of the year that they are expected to check their emails once a day as that will be your preferred method of communication. The first time a member of staff says they didn't know what was happening because they didn't check their emails, remind them of the expectations. If it's an ongoing problem, then go and see that member of staff and have the conversation:

'Hi Mark, I was just wondering if you're confident with using your emails? It's just you've missed a lot of messages over the last few weeks and it's important you know what's going on. Do you want me to show you how to check your emails?' (He'll probably say no.) 'Great OK – so can I assume there's no problem with that and you'll be checking your emails each day from now on?'

## Scenario 3: the angry parent

An angry parent is ranting and raving in the lobby. She says her child is being bullied and that the school isn't doing anything to intervene. She is demanding to see the headteacher – SLT are on an away day and, as phase leader, you are the most senior person in the school. How do you defuse the situation? The first thing to do is get the parent away from the lobby and away from the pupils. Ask them to calm down and stop shouting: 'I want to help you, but I will not have this conversation while you're shouting at me.' If they continue to shout then you can deploy the broken record technique of repeating your request until they listen: 'I want to help you, but I will not have this conversation while you're shouting at me.' If they manage to calm themselves down and want to voice their grievance, listen carefully and make notes to remind yourself of what was said. You may not be able to make any promises as to what will happen next, but what you can say is, 'I understand how worrying this is for you. I've written it all down and will be meeting with the headteacher when she's back in tomorrow morning.' Make sure you do pass the note on and follow up with the parent, either by grabbing them after school or phoning home, to update them on what's happened.

## Scenario 4: the flailing teacher

Despite sustained support, a teacher in your team hasn't improved over a period of time. He frequently arrives late, doesn't mark his books and his lesson observations haven't improved all term. One of the main problems is that his subject knowledge isn't strong enough. Your SLT want you to write a development plan with him and set some specific targets. They're talking about starting ability proceedings if he shows no evidence of improving.

Remember the situational leadership model from Chapter 2? (If not, head to page 33 now.) At this point it couldn't hurt to work out where this teacher falls on this grid:

| | |
|---|---|
| Unwilling but able | Willing but unable |
| Willing and able | Unable and unwilling |

In the scenario above it sounds as though the teacher is either willing but unable (he wants to do well but will need support to improve) or unwilling and unable, which could be more of a problem. The first thing to do is arrange a meeting with the teacher – it's perfectly reasonable to ask a member of SLT to conduct the meeting with you if you feel like you could do with that support. Just be aware that having a member of SLT in a meeting automatically makes it feel more serious to the person who has been called in. (It's your call to make.) As always, prepare your key points and opening line. For example, 'Thanks for meeting with me, James. I just wanted to catch up with you to reflect on your performance this term and to think about setting some targets to keep you on track for the next few weeks.'

Explain to him that you're going to be working with him over the next few weeks to develop his practice. (His response to this will give you a clearer idea of how willing he is.) None of the problems listed in the scenario are critical; they can all be remedied with a bit of work so make just three targets. For example:

1   To get to school for 8:30am every morning

2   To mark books regularly

3   To improve subject knowledge

Once you've set the targets, the conversation takes on a new focus and it becomes about improving rather than blaming. You can discuss what support he feels he would need to meet those targets and what he's going to take responsibility for.

Target 1 is his responsibility to sort out. Short of calling him every morning to wake him up earlier (which I have known headteachers to do) he has to be responsible for getting himself to school on time.

Target 2 will probably require some support from you. Keeping on top of marking is hard and no one does it all the time. It requires a system and a consistent routine. Model for him how to mark work with pupils in lessons or use verbal feedback. Is he in-depth marking work that can just be ticked? (Chapter 10, 'Avoiding burnout', is full of tips for managing workload if you're stuck for ideas.) Once it's clear he understands the expectations and you've given him some strategies, leave him alone for a week to give him time to get on top of things before going back to have a look at some of his exercise books.

Target 3 may require some guidance. The best way to improve subject knowledge is to read up on the subject or to watch somebody else teach it. Luckily working in a school gives you plenty of opportunities to do both. You can recommend books and send him to watch teachers teaching in that subject. In the past, I've provided teachers with KS2 workbooks to help them identify the areas of maths they need help with and to give them time to practise.

As always, set a time to follow up with both the teacher and the SLT who asked you to have the conversation. Show your SLT the agreed targets and tell them when you're going to follow up.

## Scenario 5: the eye-roller

A member of staff rolls their eyes at you in a staff meeting. When this happened to me I was so shocked I didn't know what to do, so I ignored it completely and carried on as if it hadn't happened. That evening I was moaning to my friend over dinner, who is the manager of a luxury clothing retail store and she offered some excellent advice, which I will now share with you and suggest you try if you ever find yourself in this situation:

'I've been in that situation. I ignored it during the meeting because I didn't want to draw everyone's attention to it. When the meeting was over and everyone was leaving, I said, "Oh Tara, could you just

stay behind? I need a quick word." That way, everyone knew that
her behaviour had been noticed and she was going to be pulled up
on it. I could have the conversation with her immediately but also
it was done in private. I then asked her if she was OK because I'd
noticed she was rolling her eyes and told her that in future if she
wants to discuss a decision I've made, she should come and talk
to me, as her behaviour today was unprofessional and not what
I expected from her.'

It's very easy for me to write out hypothetical scenarios and offer
my advice, but what makes difficult conversations difficult is the fact
that they aren't hypothetical. They are conversations with real people
you work with every day and perhaps even have a close friendship with.
These conversations are difficult because you know you're going to have
to say something the person doesn't want to hear. However that doesn't
mean you are being unkind or nasty – you are just doing your job. As
with anything, the more you do it the easier it becomes to keep going.

This chapter has focused a lot on the negative side of leadership but
one of the great things about having a leadership role is the opportunity
to inspire others and develop their practice, which conveniently is what
Chapter 8 is all about.

# Chapter 8
# Developing others

I originally planned for this chapter to include advice about coaching, giving feedback, team teaching, delivering INSET and mentoring. However, once I started writing, I realised that I had already covered most of these topics in detail in the other chapters – I suppose this is because leadership is fundamentally all about developing other people. Instead, in this chapter, I'm going to focus on just three methods that you can use to develop your team that may be new to you as a middle leader. The first method is planning and delivering an INSET. The second is team teaching, which means teaching with another colleague (I know in some schools this term is used to describe the positive handling of children). The third method is mentoring – including suggestions about how to mentor both NQTs and more experienced staff, which is something that you will undoubtedly be asked to do at some point in your career.

## INSET

Whilst you may not have had to deliver an INSET yourself yet, you will have undoubtedly sat through a fair few led by others. You'll know from your own experience that when INSETs are good, they leave you feeling inspired, energised and keen to get back into the classroom and put into practice what you've learnt. Conversely, when they're bad, you sit politely and only half listen, wishing you were able to go and do one of the many items on the to-do list you are writing in your head. Teachers' time is precious: the few hours between dismissing pupils and going home are often packed with running after-school clubs, marking, planning, catching up with colleagues and getting ready for the next day. So, if you're going to take up teachers' time with an INSET, it has to be worthwhile. Whilst it's easy to identify what makes a bad INSET, working out what makes an effective INSET takes a bit more thought. And it starts at the planning stage.

## Planning your INSET

A good INSET will aim to do at least one, if not a few, of the following:

- Improve staff subject knowledge
- Share new research and suggest how it could be applied in the classroom
- Share ideas
- Reflect on current practice
- Introduce new initiatives or policies
- Update staff on changes to curriculum or assessment
- Inspire staff
- Moderate children's work

Generally, you'll be asked to deliver INSET on a specific subject or theme, such as assessment or KS1 writing, or a policy that you've updated. Whatever the purpose of the INSET, you have to start by working out what your key message is going to be. Is it something practical that the rest of the staff can take straight back into class with them? Or is it some research they can read and reflect on? It could just be that you want your staff to leave the INSET with a better knowledge or understanding of your subject. Remember the pathway planning from Chapter 3 where you identify the end point and then work out the steps needed to get you to that point? Well, approach planning an INSET in a similar way: decide what it is you want the staff to take away from your INSET and then work out how to get them there. Here are some pointers to help you with your planning:

1   Delivering INSET to adults is not the same as teaching a lesson to children.

  You'll have heard people complain, 'Don't talk to me like you talk to the children.' As teachers, this is something we have to be particularly mindful of, given that we spend so much of our day talking to children. There is a difference between delivering content to adults and delivering content to children. Firstly, unlike in the classroom, you are speaking to people who are as knowledgeable and skilled as yourself, and some may be even more so. Secondly, all the adults in the room can read, so you don't need to read slide after slide of information to them. If you want to use slides in your INSET, then keep the text on them to a minimum – a few bullet points will suffice.

2   Start by explaining why you are running the INSET.

Whether it's introducing a new policy, giving feedback, sharing research or updating staff on the priorities for your department, always start with why you are doing it. For example, 'I've been thinking about how we can raise boys' attainment in reading across the school and I found this piece of research I would like to share with you' or 'As you know, one of our whole-school priorities is to improve staff wellbeing, so in today's INSET we're going to be reflecting on our own practice and discussing some strategies for managing our workload.'

3   Get the staff involved.

Your INSET does not have to be you talking for an hour. Have something for the staff to do – whether that is simply discussing what they've heard, a short paper task or just giving them time to make some notes on what they've heard. I've received some fantastic CPD that involved listening to an expert speaker talk for a full hour, but this approach is a lot of pressure to put on yourself for your first INSET and, at 5pm on a Wednesday evening, tired teachers may appreciate an activity to keep them alert! Don't feel as though you have to do all the work – you're in a room of experts who can lead discussions and suggest ideas and who want to learn.

Once you've worked out what you want to say and what you want the staff to do, it's time to put it all together and give it some shape. You don't need a long, detailed plan, but map out the rough structure you want to follow. This could just take the form of a list, for example:

- Discuss feedback from monitoring.
- Explain why we need to introduce this change or how it will help us.

- Share research/video/article.
- Teachers discuss the research in groups at their tables.
- Explore what this looks like in our school.
- Teachers plan this into their own lesson.

## The countdown to your INSET

### Two weeks before

Do your research – read up on your subject and make notes. The more evidence-based you can be, the stronger your case is. I guarantee that, whatever your topic, somebody has done some relevant research on it. Find it, read it and assess how useful it is to you, if and how it is relevant to your school, and what it might look like in your classrooms. Be selective with the research you use: look at the environment the research was conducted in and consider if it is appropriate for your school. Thousands of research papers are published about education every year and not all will be useful to you. Look at the demographic, the sample size and read any contradictory research or criticism.

### One week before

Now is the time to start putting together the resources you'll need for the INSET (e.g. making slides, printing articles, etc.) PowerPoint is a great tool, but if you feel like being a bit more adventurous there are other ways you can present your information. Prezi is great, although it can take a while to get your head around. Google Slides is very simple to use. If you fancy doing something completely different then go to www.powtoon.com and get creative!

### Three days before

Run your plan for your INSET past your line manager or a more experienced middle leader – they'll be able to offer you feedback and make some suggestions as to how it could be improved.

### One day before

Check you know how to hook your laptop up to the projector and that all the technology you need is working. Read through your slides to make sure you're happy with the content and to catch any typos. If you're feeling nervous about speaking to a group of adults, practise delivering your INSET at home in front of the mirror. The less time you spend looking at the slides the better, so take ownership of the content and make sure you know exactly what you want to say. Finally, have an early night and relax! You are well prepared and know what you're doing. (Oh and make a note to buy sweets on the way into school – everybody appreciates sweets.)

## Ten minutes before

Once you're all set up and ready to go, make yourself a cup of tea, take a few deep breaths and smile – you can do this. Stand with your back straight and head up, and greet people as they come in to the room. You're up!

- Speak clearly and slowly – more slowly than feels natural. Resist the urge to speed up and rush through things because you're nervous.

- Remember, these are your colleagues and they are on your side, so try to relax. Allow your personality to shine through and don't be afraid to use humour.

- If you've set a task for the staff to do, go around to all the groups and talk to them about what they're doing or reading and get their opinions.

- Make sure you leave time to take any questions at the end. Don't panic – you're not expected to know all the answers so don't be afraid to say, 'I'm not sure to be honest. Let me find out and get back to you.'

## After your INSET

Relax, you did it! If you used slides, upload them to your school's online platform or email them around – they will serve as a prompt to remind everyone of the key messages from your INSET and you may want to keep a copy as evidence for your performance management.

INSET is one way you can develop others, and it's the tool we use most regularly in school. The rest of this chapter will explore the other ways you can develop the members of your team whether they are an experienced teacher or an NQT.

# Developing experienced staff

Developing staff who have as much or even more experience than you do can sometimes feel slightly uncomfortable. I was 28 years old when I got my first assistant headship and had been teaching for just five years, so there were times when I would question what I had to offer a teacher who was double my age and had decades of experience. However, everybody, no matter how long they have been in the profession, is capable of improving their practice and learning from others. If you approach these strategies with humility and with an understanding that you will also learn from the person you are working with, then the experience will be equally beneficial for both parties. Let's start by looking at team teaching, sometimes referred to as co-teaching. I believe team teaching is one of the most underused tools for developing experienced staff.

## Team teaching

It is my firm belief that when team teaching is done well it is one of the most effective ways of improving a teacher's practice. As teachers, it is all too easy to get stuck in your own bubble, particularly if you work in a primary school – you have your class and your classroom, and you go in each day, close the door and teach your lessons. Occasionally you'll pop out for a cup of coffee or lunch, but you'll rarely have the chance to spend time in other teachers' classrooms or observe other members of staff, let alone teach and plan with them. As I said in Chapter 6, 'Monitoring', observing other teachers is a real privilege because it's a chance to develop your own practice and learn from your colleagues. Team teaching is even better in this sense. It is often thought of as a strategy used to improve struggling teachers, but everyone can learn something from team teaching, no matter what point they are at in their career.

## What is team teaching?

Team teaching is 'a group of two or more teachers working together to plan, conduct and evaluate the learning activities for the same group of learners.' (Goetz, 2000) You can team teach just for a one-off lesson or for a sequence of lessons, but it is most effective when it is done multiple times over consecutive weeks. I've had the most success with team teaching when I've done it on a weekly basis for half a term. The purpose is for the staff to learn from one another and, as a middle leader, you will be modelling your expectations for the class teacher you are working with.

## Planning team teaching
To ensure the team teaching process is genuinely beneficial it needs to be planned carefully. Here are some pointers:

1   Map it out.

Before you start planning the content of the lessons you will team teach, you should start by discussing which aspect (or aspects) of your practice you want to focus on and come up with a rough schedule. The focus could be subject specific (e.g. to improve maths subject knowledge) or it could be something more general (e.g. to develop behaviour management strategies for dealing with low-level behaviour). On the next page is a template you might find useful for planning a week of team teaching. Use one copy for every week you are planning to team teach (e.g. if you're doing it for six weeks, you'll need six copies). (A blank copy of this document is available to download from www.bloomsbury.com/outstanding-middle-leader.)

| Team teaching schedule | |
|---|---|
| **Week _____** | |
| Lesson objective | *Here you put the objective of the lesson, e.g. to simplify fractions.* |
| Area of focus | *This is where you put the area of development you are focusing on, e.g. behaviour management.* |
| Plan | *This will be a broad-stroke plan for the lesson you will be team teaching this week.* |
| Evaluation | *This is where you evaluate what you have learnt in the lesson after you have taught it and how it has helped you to develop your practice.* |
| Suggested area of focus for the next lesson | *Based on your evaluation it may be that you continue with the same focus or work on a new area of development.* |

**2**   Plan the lesson.

Once you start planning the lesson you'll need to decide the specific objectives you want to cover and what your area of focus will be. Make sure you're splitting the workload evenly, including dividing up the resourcing of the lesson.

This is also the time to discuss how you're going to deliver the lesson. There are plenty of different ways to do this, so I'm only going to discuss the two most commonly used models. People call these models different names, but I like to call them 'Lead and support' and 'Divide and conquer'.

Lead and support: In this model one member of staff takes the lead in delivering the lesson while the other teacher takes a more supportive role and targets particular pupils to observe and work with, as well as supporting with behaviour management. It is beneficial for you, as the more senior member of staff, to be able to take the supporting role as it puts you in a better position for reflecting on how the lesson was delivered and what the children learnt. Equally, the other member of staff will benefit from watching you lead so make sure you alternate roles over the weeks you work together.

Divide and conquer: In this model you divide the lesson up into sections and agree beforehand who is going to deliver which section. This model is more challenging, as lessons don't always break up into neat sections, so you'll need to be mindful of one another when you're teaching to try to ensure one teacher doesn't end up dominating the lesson. The benefit of this approach is that every week you can model the practice you want the member of staff you're working with to develop. For example, if they have said they want to develop their ability to deliver clear explanations, then you can make sure your own explanations are clear and concise.

Neither model is necessarily better – they both have their pros and cons, so the best thing you can do is to try them both and see which model you prefer.

**3**   Teach the lesson.

Finally, after all the discussions and planning, it's time to teach the lesson. Pop in to see the member of staff in the morning to make sure you have all the resources you need, recap on your plan and check that you're both happy with the role you will be taking during the lesson. During the lesson, if you're supporting while the other member of staff leads, make sure you're watching the pupils as much as the teacher and intervening where you think a group of pupils needs additional support. You can ask them follow-up questions and work with them, but make sure you aren't talking to them when the lead teacher is teaching because there is nothing more frustrating than trying to deliver a lesson when another member of staff is talking. Don't be afraid to intervene in the lesson if you feel it is necessary – this is not an observation; you are working together. If you're leading, make sure you're modelling best practice and make a mental note of who the supporting teacher is working with for the evaluation.

4   Evaluate it.

After the lesson, take time to sit with the member of staff and evaluate how it went. Your evaluation will guide your plan for the following week, so it's important that you both reflect honestly on the lesson. Use the following questions to guide the discussion:

- What went well?
- Which children struggled in the lesson and why? What could be done next time to make sure these children don't fall behind?
- What could have been improved?
- Which area of development do we want to focus on next week, based on how this lesson has gone?
- What did we both learn from this lesson? (Remember, it's important to show that you are also reflecting and developing your practice throughout this process.)
- Make notes during your evaluation and then leave it a few days before planning the next lesson. You'll both benefit from having time to process the last lesson and think about your priorities for the next one.

As well as being a standalone method for developing more experienced staff members, team teaching can be done in the long term as part of a mentoring programme for an experienced member of staff or an NQT. Whilst there is an automatic mentoring programme put in place for NQTs in their first year, mentoring is rarely used with staff who have been teaching for a while, despite the fact it can be highly effective. In one school I worked in every member of staff, including the headteacher, had a mentor who was their person to go to for support, ideas and ongoing professional development. Let's have a look in more detail at how that can work.

## Mentoring experienced staff

A mentor is defined as 'an experienced and expert teacher who takes on the additional role of supporting and developing colleagues.' (Wright, 2012) It is a term that is often mistakenly used to mean 'coach', but the two are in fact very different. The key difference is that a coach does not need to be an expert in the same field as the person they are coaching, whereas a mentor requires the knowledge and skills of the profession that the mentee is working in. Mentoring is not necessarily just for teachers who are struggling: we all have room for improvement and mentoring can be used to really stretch and challenge your most skilled teachers.

Mentoring an experienced member of staff can feel like a daunting prospect, particularly if they have been teaching longer than you. However, if you approach it with humility and an acknowledgement that you, the mentor, stand to benefit from working with the mentee too, then you'll find the process hugely rewarding. Mentoring should be a temporary intervention, whether it is for six weeks, six months or a year. At the start of the process you should decide on some targets: these could be subject specific (e.g. develop strategies for supporting weaker readers) or they could be something broader (e.g. to create a more manageable system for marking). An NQT may need more general support, but with a more experienced teacher it's important to really focus in on the specific areas they want to work on. It's also important to remember the following:

1   Mentoring should not add to the mentee's workload.

Having a mentor should not be an additional pressure on your mentee's time. If it is, then the stress of trying to fit everything in will negate any of the benefits of being mentored. If you want your mentee to go and observe another teacher, then release them from class to do so – don't ask that they do it in their PPA time. Don't ask for written evaluations of lessons or weekly diaries reflecting on their lessons. Your school may require you to fill in some paperwork as part of the mentoring programme to track targets, but try to take this on yourself and avoid passing it on to your mentee.

2 Keep weekly meetings informal.

Have a weekly meeting with your mentee that is no longer than 15 minutes to check in and see how their week is going. This is not a formal meeting – you're checking in with them to find out how they are, answer any questions and just offer your general ongoing support.

3 Don't over-observe.

It can be tempting to book in weekly observations and set a new target after each one is achieved, but this is not the best approach. Give your mentee space between observations to develop their own practice without the pressure of being watched. You may find that giving your mentee opportunities to observe others or team teach is actually more beneficial than repeatedly observing them.

4 Celebrate success.

As teachers we're great at praising children on a daily basis but, for some reason, we're not so good at praising adults. When you see something good in your mentee's practice, tell them! Celebrate every success no matter how small. Show them that you're learning from them throughout the process.

## When to stop mentoring

The process of setting targets, observing, team teaching and meeting weekly can continue for as long as you and your mentee feel that it is beneficial. Once you're both happy that the mentee has met their targets and achieved what they set out to achieve, then there is no need for the mentoring to continue. Often a member of SLT will ask to observe the mentee at the end of the mentoring to see what progress has been made.

They may also ask to speak with you both about how you've found the process.

# Developing an NQT

You can use all the techniques above to help develop an NQT, but mentoring an NQT is slightly different from mentoring a more experienced member of staff. Let's take a look.

## Mentoring an NQT

Being asked to mentor an NQT is a fantastic opportunity for your own professional development, but it's also a huge responsibility and it will add to your workload so make sure, before you commit, that you have the time and resources available to do the job properly. It's no exaggeration to say that an NQT mentor can make or break an NQT. As a mentor, you will define what your NQT's first year of teaching is like. Ideally, the NQT mentor–mentee relationship will be supportive, positive and beneficial to both parties. However, it can sometimes be a tricky relationship to manage, partly because it's an imbalanced one. The mentee is less senior to the mentor and it's likely that, as the mentor, you have a number of other responsibilities and mentoring is just one of them, which means that the mentee might not always be your top priority, even if the mentee is relying heavily on the partnership. Finally, the NQT mentor has to assess the mentee's performance over the year, which might mean that the NQT feels as though they cannot be honest if they are struggling, for fear that any confessions will be used against them in a report or assessment. To overcome this, you need to have honest, clear communication and a strong working relationship based on trust.

What does being an NQT mentor actually entail? Ultimately your job is to ensure that by the end of the year, there is evidence to show the NQT has met all of the teaching standards and can competently plan and deliver lessons. The actual to-do list looks something like this:

- Offering support and encouragement
- Observing lessons and giving feedback

- Writing a termly report on the NQT's performance and setting and reviewing termly targets (see page 118)
- Team teaching
- Meeting regularly with the NQT both formally and informally (ideally at least once a week)
- Arranging training or external CPD opportunities for the NQT (in discussion with your SLT)

The amount of support the NQT will require will vary depending on the training they've had, their confidence and their own experiences and expectations of the job. The step from student to NQT is big: they are responsible for setting up a classroom and establishing routines from scratch, rather than just maintaining somebody else's. I once described my NQT year as being like passing your driving test and then getting into your own car and realising that your driving instructor had been using dual control the whole time. A worrying statistic for you: four in ten NQTs quit within a year (Weale, 2015). So what can you do, as a mentor, to make that first year as smooth as possible for your NQT? For starters, you should do everything on the list above but here are some further suggestions:

1 Be available.

   As I have already mentioned, you still have your own class and your leadership responsibilities, but try to put some time aside every day to check in with your NQT. It doesn't have to be for long – popping your head around the door in the morning will be fine most days. Book in a longer meeting once a week to find out how their week has gone and discuss any opportunities for professional development they would like.

2 Be a positive, professional role model.

   Try to avoid saying things like, 'This will be the hardest year of your professional life.' This person is new to the profession – they're likely to be enthusiastic, if not slightly idealistic, about what lies ahead so be positive. The first year of teaching doesn't need to be the hardest. That's not to say you shouldn't prepare the NQT for the pressures they'll face, but you can do this without doom-mongering. Secondly, model having a positive and professional approach to your NQT. Greet them in the morning with a smile on your face, dressed the part, organised and ready for the day. If you are feeling overwhelmed or stressed, don't burden your mentee with it – find a more experienced member of staff to share that with.

**3**   Be pro-active.

If you've spotted an area of practice that your NQT needs to work on, be proactive. Arrange for them to go and observe other members of staff or even arrange for them to visit another school to get some ideas. Don't wait for them to come to you or, even worse, for a member of your SLT to come to you and ask what you've been doing to support your NQT.

**4**   You're not creating a mini-me.

Your job is to support your NQT in becoming a skilled, knowledgeable professional. You are not trying to make them like you. They have to discover their own style of teaching and find out what works for them so be aware of your own biases and give your mentee plenty of space to try things out. That's not to say you can't make suggestions or guide them – after all, that is the role of the mentor – but you're *making suggestions*, not insisting they copy the way you do things.

**5**   Don't be a helicopter mentor.

You'll no doubt have encountered the helicopter parents: they're overprotective and focus in on their children's lives with excruciating detail. The term 'helicopter' refers to the notion that they can often be seen hovering over their children. You will not be able to stop your NQT from making mistakes or feeling stressed – that is not your job. Your job is to make sure they learn from their mistakes and help them develop strategies for coping with stress. As tempting as it might be, it is not your job to plan your mentee's lessons for them, do their marking or take on their workload – your job is to help them manage their workload themselves.

## The NQT report

At the end of each term it is your job to write a report on the NQT you are mentoring. In my opinion, writing the termly NQT report is the least interesting part of being an NQT mentor. The report is submitted to the local authority as evidence that the NQT is receiving the support they are entitled to and that they are meeting the teaching standards set by the Department for Education. Each local authority has its own version of the report and this will be provided to you to complete, but, in general, it's a very dense document that has to be completed in a very specific way. If it isn't up to scratch, it will be sent back for improvement, so it's worth getting right first time. The purpose of the report is to collate all the evidence you've collected over the term about the NQT's progress and achievements. You'll then need to use this evidence to prove the NQT has met each of the individual teaching standards.

Before you start writing, make sure you have all the following information to hand:

- Lesson observation feedback from others who have observed the NQT and your own notes
- A list of your NQT's contributions to wider school life (e.g. running clubs, attending extra-curricular events, etc.)
- Attendance and punctuality data
- Assessment data for their class
- The NQT's completed end-of-term questionnaire
- The targets that were set at the beginning of the term
- Notes from book scrutiny, pupil interviews and any other monitoring you've done

As you go through each standard, find the most relevant piece of evidence for each section and explain how it shows the NQT has met that standard. At the end of each section you have to set a new target for the following term. For more advice about setting SMART targets head over to Chapter 3, 'Policies and plans'.

It's helpful to have a meeting with the NQT prior to writing the report to see how they feel the term has gone. You might find it useful to use the template review form on page 120 to make notes during this meeting. Alternatively, just ask the NQT to fill it in themselves so you have it to refer to. It also gives the NQT an opportunity to feed back on the support they have received to date. You can download a copy of this form from www.bloomsbury.com/outstanding-middle-leader.

---

### NQT termly review

**Name:**                                    **Term: Autumn/Spring/Summer**

Think back over the last term – which of your achievements are you most proud of?

What would you like your targets to be next term?

Have you run any clubs or extra-curricular activities this term?

What CPD have you received this term? (Just the name of the course or subject of the course will suffice.)

What further training do you feel would be beneficial next term?

Is there anything else we could provide you with that would help you do your job more effectively?

Is there anything else you would like us to know about your experiences from this term?

---

Mentoring another member of staff is incredibly hard work and comes with a demanding workload, but it can be hugely rewarding and is a fantastic way to develop your leadership skills and show your SLT you're capable of taking on further responsibility. Developing others is an integral part of your role as a middle leader. You'll draw great satisfaction from seeing members of staff in your team flourish under your leadership – it really is one of the best parts of the job. So, hold on to that fuzzy, warm feeling as we approach Chapter 9, which is about one part of the job that doesn't leave school leaders with quite such a warm glow. Yes, we need to talk about Ofsted.

# Chapter 9
# An inspector calls

I didn't intend to write an entire chapter about Ofsted. When I first put together the book proposal, this chapter wasn't going to be in it because I believe that the way we lead, work and teach should not be influenced by Ofsted. We don't work for Ofsted and we aren't motivated by their judgements. However, once I started writing, I spoke to a few new middle leaders and they said they would find it useful to have a breakdown of what to expect during an Ofsted inspection. If you haven't gone through an Ofsted inspection as a middle leader, you won't know that there are things that will be expected of you that were not expected of you when you were a class teacher. For example, it is likely that you will be interviewed or you might be asked to produce certain pieces of evidence or data and, most importantly, you'll have a team to support and coach throughout the inspection. For these reasons, I decided that a chapter on Ofsted would be useful after all. So, here you have it – a chapter all about what you can expect when the inspectors call. At the end of the chapter are some myths about Ofsted (if you only read one section of this chapter, make it that one). The myths about Ofsted's expectations have been used to justify all sorts of ridiculous policies and initiatives in schools over the last few years, despite the fact that Ofsted have released several myth-busting documents.

So, please take this chapter as it is intended – practical advice for the things you may have to do as a middle leader during an inspection. Don't let it set the agenda in your department or influence your day-to-day practice.

# What to expect when you're expecting ... 'The Call'

As a general rule, 'Good' or 'Outstanding' schools are inspected once every five years. If you're working in a school that has been graded 'Requires Improvement', then inspections are more frequent and probably occur every two to three years. Headteachers will typically start saying that they're 'expecting The Call' around the third inspection-free year. During this time, speculation will turn to who has recently had 'The Call' and what it might mean for your school: 'Have you heard? Two schools down the road have had "The Call" in the last week, which means we should expect it any day now', 'My friend's aunt's second cousin is an Ofsted inspector and she says that they're prioritising schools in our area', or 'Interestingly the last three inspections I know of were all at schools where the headteacher drove a silver car – and guess what colour my car is!' These statements are only mild exaggerations. Waiting for 'The Call' can be all consuming and, if you're not careful, a school can be on tenterhooks for years because they believe Ofsted are looming.

# When you get 'The Call'

Inevitably you will get 'The Call' at some point. It'll probably be when your headteacher is up a mountain in Wales with half of Year 6 or your SENCO is away at a conference. Whenever it happens, your school will have a plan of action. It's likely that all the children will be ushered into a surprise assembly while the staff are summoned to the staffroom. Once the news is out, phone calls are made to loved ones to say you'll be late home, takeaways are ordered, childcare arrangements are made, and family and friends are roped into coming in to help. You'll see empathetic husbands, wives and children coming in after work to back display boards and cut out resources. Parents, partners and friends turn up to help tidy book corners, prepare resources and make coffee. Well wishes, flowers and sometimes doughnuts will appear from neighbouring schools and old members of staff. All differences and niggles are put aside as everyone pulls together for the sake of the school. The most enjoyable aspect of the 24 hours before an Ofsted inspection is the 'Blitz spirit' that takes hold – it's an incredible bonding experience.

As I'm sure you can imagine – or know first-hand – the 24 hours between getting the call and Ofsted arriving are the most intense, hysterical and exhausting you'll ever experience when working in a school. Moods swing unpredictably between anxious and stressed but incredibly focused to completely hysterical and giddy. Before my first Ofsted inspection in 2011 I had a lightsaber battle with the headteacher (using rolls of backing paper, obviously, because real lightsabers aren't really allowed in schools).

In this time, it's important to look after yourself. Yes, there will be doughnuts and a takeaway but try to eat a couple of vegetables and drink plenty of water. Oh, and please get some sleep. It can be tempting to work into the small hours making sure everything is perfect but there's no point having every display board perfect if you have only had three hours' sleep and can't think straight on the day. Make a list of the things that *really* need doing and set a cut-off time to leave work and have a good night's sleep. As a middle leader, there will be people relying on you for support through the inspection and you won't be able to support them or be the best version of yourself if you're running on empty.

The support your team will require from you will vary depending on your role. If you're a subject leader, send a quick email with a few key reminders based on your last round of observations, e.g. 'Please make sure your targets are up to date and remember to model the task to the class.' If you're a phase leader, it might be worth getting your team together for a ~~short meeting~~ cup of tea and a bit of moral support. Some members of staff might want you to check through their lesson plans or just bounce ideas off you. If there's an NQT in your department, make time to pop into their classroom and ask if they need any help – as an NQT your first Ofsted inspection can be quite overwhelming, and it can be difficult to know where to start.

Make sure there are people supporting you too, whether that's your SLT or fellow middle leaders – find someone you can go to in those moments of stress. You cannot support others if you yourself don't feel supported.

## Things to have to hand

There was a time, not too long ago, in education, where the key to a successful Ofsted was ring binders – dozens of clearly labelled, neatly organised ring binders full of pieces of paper stored in plastic wallets. These folders were supposedly evidence that your school was 'Good' or 'Better'. Thankfully, things have changed a bit in the last few years and there is no need to bury an Ofsted inspector in paperwork. However, there are some documents you might want to have to hand for your own reference during an inspection. Whether or not you keep them in a neatly organised ring binder is really up to you.

- The school improvement plan: You'll be expected to know the whole-school priorities and be able to explain how the work you are doing in your department fits into the school improvement plan, e.g. 'Raising attainment of free-school-meals pupils is a whole-school priority at the moment and, as KS1 leader, I've introduced the following targeted interventions for all pupil premium children in my phase.'

- Your action plan: Annotate this with where you are in meeting the targets you set. Don't panic if you haven't met any of your targets yet – just be ready to talk about what you've done so far and the impact it has had.

- Any policies to do with your area: E.g. subject policy, teaching and learning policy, marking policy and behaviour policy.

- Up-to-date attainment and progress data for your subject, phase or year group: Find your assessment coordinator and ask them for the headlines from the data, e.g. current attainment and progress and any discrepancies between groups.

- Last year's attainment and progress data: This will be useful for drawing comparisons and showing the impact that you've had as a middle leader.

- Your notes and the key headlines from your most recent round of monitoring: E.g. book scrutiny, observations and pupil surveys.

## The interview

The word 'interview' is not really an accurate description of this conversation – it's more like a discussion. The inspector isn't trying to catch you out and there won't be any trick questions. They are just trying to find out what you know about your department and what impact you've had as a middle leader. The following is a list of some of the questions you *might* be asked by an Ofsted inspector. I collated this list based on questions that I have been asked in Ofsted interviews and through talks with fellow middle leaders about their experiences. It is by no means exhaustive and you may find your experiences with Ofsted to be entirely different so treat this as a rough guide.

The important thing to remember during an inspection is that *you* are the expert in this situation, not the Ofsted inspector; you know your school and your pupils far better than they do. This is your chance to tell them about all the fantastic things you have been working on and present the evidence that shows what a positive impact you've had. Be honest about the challenges you've faced and what you've done to overcome them. If there's something they haven't asked about, but you want to draw to their attention, just tell them. Finally, if you don't know an answer then don't try to make something up – it isn't a test – just say, 'I'm afraid I don't actually have that information at the moment but I can certainly get it for you after this meeting or find someone who will know to talk to you.'

1  How well do pupils achieve in your subject or phase?

Undoubtedly, there will be questions about progress and achievement. You won't be expected to recall every piece of data off the top of your head, but it is worth knowing the headlines, e.g. '76 per cent of pupils met or exceeded National Expectations last year. Looking at this year's data 82 per cent of pupils are on track to meet or exceed National Expectations and 94 per cent of pupils are making expected progress.' Talk about how attainment and progress in your school compares to the national picture. In 2017 the percentage of pupils nationally reaching the expected level or better were:

- Reading: 71 per cent
- Writing: 76 per cent
- English, grammar, punctuation and spelling (EGPS): 77 per cent
- Maths: 75 per cent (For Schools Education Service, 2017)

2  What are the strengths and weaknesses in your subject or phase? How do you know this?

Share a couple of strengths, but don't try to cover too many. Make sure they genuinely are strengths and that you have the evidence to back up your claims, e.g. 'The quality of teaching in my department is consistently 'good' or 'better' – this is evidenced in the children's work and their high levels of attainment.' Be honest about the weaknesses – choose one target from your action plan and explain why you set it and what you intend to do.

**3**   What is staff morale like in the school and how do you know?

This is an interesting question. I'm of the opinion that if you have any major grievances about the way the school is run you either raise them with your SLT directly or accept you cannot change things and leave. I wouldn't use an interview with an Ofsted inspector as a forum for airing my gripes. However, if you genuinely feel as though there is something Ofsted should know about how the staff are treated, don't feel like you can't say it – just make sure you've voiced it to your SLT beforehand.

**4**   What are your key priorities for improvement?

At this point you can produce your beautifully annotated action plan. Explain why you chose the targets and what you've done so far to meet them. It doesn't matter if you haven't ticked everything off your plan yet. Just talk about what you've done and, once again, the impact it's had, e.g.:

'When I first started as geography leader there were real gaps in staff subject knowledge and, as a result, some areas of the curriculum were not covered or taught properly. I introduced a new scheme of work at the beginning of the academic year. I started using it in my own classroom and then delivered a series of INSETs modelling how it should be used throughout the rest of the school. I've been team teaching this term and the scheme has already had a positive impact. If you look at the quality of the children's work and speak to them they show a greater understanding of the concepts than they have done in the past.'

**5**   What impact have the changes you've implemented had on attainment and how do you know?

All this question means is, 'Have the things you've implemented improved the pupils' grades and how do you know?' It's worth having both the current data and last year's KS1 and KS2 results to hand. Show the inspector last year's attainment and progress and compare it with where the pupils are now, e.g. 'I introduced X, Y and Z and as a result attainment increased by eight per cent on last year.' If it's too early in the year to be able to draw any firm conclusions from the data then you can be honest and say, 'We don't yet have enough data to compare with last year's, but from the evidence we have got I can confidently say ...' If you find yourself in the situation where your data is showing slow progress or no progress at all (unlikely, but possible) then the important thing is that you make it clear that you've identified the issue and you explain what you're doing about it, e.g. 'The changes we have made have not yet impacted on the data in the way we had hoped. One possible explanation for this is ... and our plan going forward is ...'

**6**   How has the school furthered your professional development?

Here you can talk about any training you've received from the school. This could be INSET or external courses, team teaching, mentoring or coaching, visits to other schools and observing colleagues. If you can't think of a specific example, then you can talk about your ambitions for the future and how your school is helping you work to achieve them, e.g. 'I'm hoping to apply for an assistant headship in the next few years and my school is providing me with the experiences I'll need to do this.'

**7**   Are there any gaps in achievement between different groups of pupils, e.g. gender, SEN, EAL and looked after children, and what are you doing to close them?

The groups you need to be aware of are SEN pupils, pupils with English as an additional language, different ethnic groups, pupils in care, children from military families and gender. Speak to your assessment coordinator and get the headlines. You'll need to explain where the gaps are and what you're doing to narrow them.

**8**   How do you assess learning and progress in your department?

This question is about how you collect assessment data and what you do with it. Since levels were scrapped in 2016, schools have had to come up with their own method of assessing pupil progress. It doesn't really matter what the system is as long as you can explain it clearly and show that you understand how the data is used, e.g.:

'We do formal assessments at the end of each term and the raw scores are converted into a one, two or three, which stands for 'working towards', 'meeting' or 'exceeding National Expectations'. Each term we use the data to help us choose the children for interventions and to inform the teacher's planning for the next term.'

**9** Tell us about the achievement of pupil premium pupils in your phase or subject.

Pupil premium money is given to schools to support pupils from poorer backgrounds and provide them with a free school meal. It's important that you know about the gaps between groups and can talk about what you've put in place to support them, e.g.:

'After our assessments in January we identified that our pupil premium boys were falling behind in writing. One way we tackled this was by working with the class teachers on improving the quality of the teaching of writing and targeting pupils on free school meals with tailored interventions during lessons. Our results from the spring term show that the gap is slowly closing although there is more work to be done.'

**10** How often do you carry out monitoring in your phase or subject?

Talk about all the different types of monitoring you do, e.g. pupil interviews, lesson observations, book looks, data analysis, etc. Explain the processes you go through and how you share the findings of monitoring with the rest of your department. Don't forget to mention the informal monitoring you do, e.g. drop-ins and learning walks – these all count!

**11** What is the quality of teaching like in your department and how do you know?

Talk about the lesson observations you've carried out and what you've learnt from them. Try to be as specific as you can, e.g.:

'The teaching of reading is a real strength in my department and this is evident in both observations and the data. We identified a gap in staff's subject knowledge in the autumn term when the new grammar curriculum was introduced, so we've been focusing on this aspect. We've delivered a series of INSETs and I've been team teaching grammar lessons with staff who require support. It's already improved but we're still working on it.'

If you have a teacher who is on an improvement plan, don't be afraid of saying so. Ofsted will want to know what you're doing to improve teaching. As long as you can explain what's been put in place to support this member of staff you have nothing to worry about.

**12** How do the governors stay up to date with what is going on in your phase or subject?

Different schools have different approaches to working with the governors. Some host annual events where they invite the governors in to observe lessons and spend the day with a class. Others link each governor to a subject or phase and they keep in touch with the middle leaders via email. The headteacher writes a termly report about what's been happening in the school for the governors, which, as a middle leader, you may be asked to contribute to. Finally, you may also be asked to attend a governors' meeting and give a short presentation on what you've been working on. All this question requires is for you to explain clearly and concisely your relationship with the governors and how you keep them informed about your work.

**13** What does your SLT do to look after the wellbeing of staff?

As the teacher shortage continues, there is a greater focus on what schools are doing to retain their staff. Most schools want to look after their staff and have been trying to find ways to ease stress and reduce workload. From more flexible marking policies to termly duvet days, now is the time to share everything your school does to look after you. (For more advice on promoting wellbeing in your school head to Chapter 10.) If you think your school isn't doing enough for staff wellbeing, you can voice this but phrase it carefully and professionally, e.g. 'Obviously teaching is always going to be a stressful job with a large workload. I do think my school are concerned about the wellbeing of their staff, but they probably could be doing a bit more to support us.'

# Myths about Ofsted

It's not clear how these myths have been perpetuated. Are they passed around on pieces of paper at headteacher conferences? Or is there one big game of Chinese whispers going on from school to school about what Ofsted want? These myths are damaging. They have been used to justify all sorts of policies that haven't actually helped children make progress and have made teachers' lives harder. There are inconsistencies between Ofsted inspectors, but we can change that. Spread the word far and wide: photocopy these pages and put them in your staffroom, leave them on your headteachers' desk or print them onto a t-shirt and wear it every day. Because the only way we are going to be able to dispel these myths is by confronting them head on. Here we go:

1   Ofsted grade lessons.

   I think this myth has been killed off, but if it is still haunting your school then here you have it: Ofsted do not grade individual lessons and they don't expect you to either. Officially, Ofsted haven't graded individual lessons since 2014. Ofsted grade the quality of teaching across the whole school and they make their decision by observing lessons, looking at children's work and the data. They'll ask you, as a middle leader, how you know what teaching in your department is like and use your monitoring to feed into their decision making. Teachers will be offered the opportunity to receive feedback on their lesson but it won't be a grade.

2   Ofsted want to see children responding to marking.

   This myth is like a cockroach. It refuses to die. I swear, if the world ends tomorrow with a nuclear war, somewhere a survivor will be muttering about Ofsted wanting to see children's responses to marking. It's not true. Ofsted just want to see the school's marking policy being followed.

It's hard to pinpoint the exact moment when marking went from being a task that could be completed on the bus ride home to an activity that requires three different-coloured pens, a variety of stamps and stickers, and a good five hours. Marking has always been part of teaching, and always will be, but these marking policies are examples of marking on steroids. I think it started around 2012 when Ofsted announced it would no longer form judgements about teaching based on 20-minute showpiece lessons (hurrah!) and would instead use children's exercise books to build a picture of what happens in that classroom on a day-to-day basis.

The problem with using the books to judge progress is that it means progress in books has to be evident at *any point in the year*. And how do you show progress in books if Ofsted arrive on 8th September? The solution we as a profession came up with was next step comments. At the end of each lesson go through each child's work, pull out a part that they didn't get right or need to develop and set them a follow-up question or task that will help them improve. This evolved into elaborate marking policies that meant using three different types of pen, setting the pupil a task or question to answer based on their work, giving them time to respond and then, as if you didn't have enough on your plate already, *going back and responding to the children's response.* Double- and sometimes triple-marked work has become the norm in schools across the country and it's not only damaging – it's also completely unnecessary. Ofsted want to see that the marking is in line with the marking policy. That's it. They want to see that what the school says is happening is actually happening.

3   Ofsted want to see lesson plans.

In their own words: 'Ofsted does not require schools to provide individual lesson plans to inspectors. Equally, Ofsted does not require schools to provide previous lesson plans.' (Ofsted, 2018) If your school is insisting you print off your planning and keep it in a folder for Ofsted, you should draw their attention to this page or the Ofsted myth busting document: www.gov.

uk/government/publications/school-inspection-handbook-
from-september-2015/ofsted-inspections-mythbusting. Ofsted
don't need to see the plans for the lessons you're planning to
teach during the inspection or the planning you did last week.
While we're on it, you don't need to re-plan once you've had
the Ofsted call – just teach what you already had planned. It
was this philosophy that saw me delivering a lesson dressed as a
bear during my first Ofsted inspection (we'd planned a fairy tale
dress-up day and I'd already got my costume sorted). In some
ways, being dressed as a bear lightened the experience, although
it is by no means necessary for you to follow suit.

**4**   Ofsted inspectors prefer a certain teaching style.

From guided groups, lolly sticks to mini-plenaries and five-
way differentiation, you name it, it's been written as a school
policy out of the belief that it's what Ofsted want to see. Ofsted
inspectors should not show a preference for a particular method
or style. Don't feel pressured into teaching a certain way just
because you're being observed. Just do what you normally do –
do what works.

**5**   Ofsted want to see a certain amount of work.

'Ofsted want to see three pieces of maths and English in books
each week' or 'Ofsted will want evidence in books of weekly RE
lessons.' No, they don't. Please don't let any member of your
SLT convince you otherwise. Inspectors do not expect to see a
'particular frequency or quantity of work in pupils' books or
folders. Ofsted recognises that the amount of work in books and
folders will depend on the subject being studied and the age and
ability of the pupils.' (Ofsted, 2018)

**6**   Ofsted want everyone teaching the same subjects at the same
time in the same way.

I would argue that there is no word more grossly misinterpreted in
education today than 'consistency'. It has been used to justify some
terrible policies that have increased workload and had no impact
on children's learning. It started when the word 'consistency' first
began appearing in the Ofsted inspection handbook (Ofsted,
2015) – but what does the handbook actually say? Well, the

current handbook uses the word just twice. Firstly, 'Teachers have consistently high expectations of all pupils' attitudes to learning.' Secondly, '[Teachers] manage pupils' behaviour highly effectively with clear rules that are consistently enforced.'

So, for teaching and learning to be judged as 'Outstanding' in your school, if that is your ambition, then two of the criteria you have to meet are that rules are consistently enforced and teachers have consistently high expectations. That seems fair enough. That doesn't mean all the teachers teaching the same thing in the same way at the same time. As I explained in point two, what matters to Ofsted is that what happens in the school every day is consistent with what the policies say should be happening. So, if a school's policy is, 'Every teacher marks in green, purple and yellow, and the pupils respond in pink and blue, and all staff wear a silly hat on Tuesdays', then that's what they want to see.

It's all very well Ofsted releasing myth busting documents, but as long as these comments keep appearing in Ofsted inspectors' reports, these myths aren't going to disappear. Every school I've worked in, apart from where I currently work, has at some point adopted a version of the pupil response marking policy and I don't blame them. When I was researching this section of the book I spent a long time reading through Ofsted reports and in that time I found reference to frequency and thoroughness of marking in all but two of them. Ofsted themselves say, 'Ofsted does not expect to see any specific frequency, type or volume of marking and feedback' (Ofsted, 2018). Hopefully in time this message will filter down to all of their inspectors. In the meantime, you can find Sean Harford, the National Director of Ofsted, on Twitter at @HarfordSean and he's always happy to field any questions you might have about an inspection and bust any stubborn myths.

# Chapter 10
# Avoiding burnout

Back in 2011 I went to see the film *Bridesmaids* with my lovely friend Kirsty. Going to the cinema is one of my absolute favourite things to do and I'd been looking forward to seeing this film for months. We bought our popcorn, settled into our seats and the lights went down. An hour later I woke up. I'd missed over half the film. I've also only seen half of *The Wolf of Wall Street*, *Dallas Buyers Club* and *The Revenant*. Thankfully, I have some very patient friends and family who still go to the cinema with me, despite my narcoleptic tendencies.

The truth is, most teachers have an anecdote like this. Jim Smith, the author of *The Lazy Teacher's Handbook* (2017), tells the story of waking up in an Indian restaurant having missed the entire dinner, much to the amusement of his friends and fellow diners. My husband fell asleep in the Palm House on a family day out to Kew Gardens. In every staffroom I've ever worked in a teacher has fallen asleep at lunchtime at some point in the year. Being a middle leader is hugely rewarding but it is also really hard work. It's a 50- to 60-hour week, only half of which is actually spent teaching, and if you're not careful it can eat into the rest of your life both mentally and physically – whether exercise books and resources have taken over your lounge and kitchen table, you're worrying about SATs results or your concerns about Ahmed's home life are keeping you awake at 2am. It's also, without a doubt, the best job in the world and in order to do it well you need to make sure you look after yourself. This is much easier said than done. I've seen teachers drag themselves in when they probably should have been at the doctor. When my husband was a Year 6 teacher he broke his leg in the playground during SATs week and was back in school the next day to invigilate the maths paper. If you don't look after yourself and you don't try to manage your workload, you risk burnout.

# Two hats

In the first school I worked in we had a phrase that summed up the challenge faced by middle leaders: we'd say they had 'two hats'. The first was your class teacher hat and the responsibilities that came with it included: delivering lessons, marking, planning, attending INSET, writing reports, parents' evening, running clubs, setting homework, submitting data. As a middle leader, you have a second hat that comes with its own set of extra responsibilities: monitoring, setting improvement targets, looking at data, observing lessons. But here's the secret: the hats are not the same size. Your class teacher hat is bigger than your leadership hat and, whilst there will be many times in the school year where you find yourself wearing your leadership hat more often, for most of the year your class must be your first priority.

Use the school calendar in the next chapter to help you juggle wearing your two hats. Have a look and work out the times you're likely to be out of class and the times your class will need more from you. I've included some suggestions as to when you might want to write your action plan, carry out monitoring, etc., but ultimately it's up to you to decide that with your SLT.

I wholeheartedly believe that being a middle leader is one of the most difficult jobs in the school. It's a balancing act of responsibilities and requires excellent diplomacy skills. If you've been promoted in a school that you've worked at for a while you'll suddenly find yourself observing and offering feedback to your closest friends or allies and it can sometimes feel as though you're in no man's land – neither class teacher nor SLT. I don't say that to put you off – the job is as rewarding as it is challenging, but I told you I'd be honest.

As is often the case, advice like this is all too easy to dispense and not so easy to take on board, but there are a few simple and practical things you can do to make your workload more manageable. Let's start with the crux of the problem: marking.

# Managing marking

Marking is the bane of a teacher's life. You can never keep on top of it and you can never give every pupil's work the time or attention it deserves. If you even spend just two minutes marking every child's book and they do four or five lessons a day, that's four or five hours of marking a day. But there are things you can do to make it easier and schools are finding more and more ingenious ways of speeding the process up.

In 2015 the Department for Education summoned our brightest and best teachers, consultants and educationalists and commissioned them to carry out a review of teachers' workload. The findings can be found in their report, 'Eliminating unnecessary workload around marking'. Having scrutinised marking policies, the Workload Review team concluded that marking should be underpinned by three key principles. It should be: meaningful, manageable and motivating (Department for Education, 2016b).

Most of us know what meaningful marking looks like. We've experienced the satisfaction of a child being able to tackle an area of learning that they had previously struggled with as a result of our feedback. Meaningful marking motivates children to make progress. So that leaves 'manageable'. How can we make marking manageable, particularly now that so many marking policies seem to require an arsenal of stationery?

How to make marking manageable may well be the million-dollar question, but it's one we need to start addressing. A third of teachers who qualified in 2010 have already left the profession, with 50 per cent of them stating workload as one of the key reasons (Department for Education, 2014). So schools need to start taking the issue of teacher workload seriously. And there are some things you can do as a middle leader that will help those in your team.

## Plan your marking

One of the greatest challenges I faced as a middle leader was juggling my role as a full-time class teacher with my leadership responsibilities. In an attempt to maintain some sanity, I created planning rotas for maths and English. They weren't always kept to, but more often than not I could get all my marking done 7am – 8:30am and 3:30pm – 6:00pm at school. Other than test papers, I never took marking home at the weekends.

Make planning for marking part of your weekly PPA session. Look at the week ahead and the lessons you have planned. Then look at your diary and consider everything you're doing next week: clubs, INSET, parent workshops, staff meetings, social events (yes, they count).

Now look back at your lesson plans. If one of the lessons requires you to have marked the first drafts of your class's stories in detail, don't pencil that first draft lesson in for Monday when you have both INSET and dance club. Schedule heavy marking days in and write them in your diary so you know not to take on too many extra-curricular activities on those days.

Obviously your marking plan should not guide the learning and sometimes  work will have to be done on a day when it'll be difficult to get it marked but, for the most part, you can plan your marking so that it is manageable.

## Verbal feedback

Marking is just one of a variety of types of feedback and arguably it is not even the most effective for some pieces of work. Verbal feedback allows for a dialogue. The child can explain to you exactly what they did not understand and you can respond immediately. You or the child can make notes in the child's book as you feed back, so that they have a few prompts to guide them once they return to work. Verbal feedback can happen one-to-one during the lesson or, having looked at their books, by taking a small group who made similar mistakes last lesson and going through their work with them.

## Live marking

Live marking is similar to verbal feedback, but it can be done with the whole class. This works well with grammar exercises, calculations and short-answer questions. The questions go up on the board and you go through them one by one, occasionally choosing a pair of children to explain the answer or the method. The children can mark their own work as they go and add in their own corrections. The advantage of live marking is that you can mark a whole set of books during the lesson and it gives the children the chance to discuss the answer and ask questions about the things they didn't understand. Bear in mind that this sort of marking takes time. We're talking ten or 15 minutes of the lesson. If you were to mark like this every lesson, children would not produce enough work for marking to be an issue in the first place. But, if used occasionally, it can be a very effective method.

## Peer marking

You have to train your class to be able to peer mark. You'll have to model it for them, show them the sorts of comments you expect to see and for a while you'll have to give them feedback on their feedback but, once it's an established part of your class routine, it can be very valuable. I've seen effective peer marking in Year 2 and even peer critique in Year 1 – this is where children go around and say what they like and what could be improved about the work on their table. Peer marking can work with the same sort of tasks as live marking: short answers that are either right or wrong. When it comes to more complex investigations or extended pieces of writing, the quality of peer marking relies too heavily on the pupil's knowledge.

A little tip: in the first week of a new school year, mark a piece of shared writing as a class and as you're doing this create a 'Class marking policy'. This could be an agreed list of symbols that you can all use. Keep those symbols on the wall all year and the children can then use this marking policy during peer marking.

## Whole-class feedback

This method works better with KS2. Instead of marking each book and correcting every mistake, read a sample of your pupils' work – maybe half the books – and, as you read, make notes about the common errors you find (e.g. commonly misspelt words, grammatical errors and misconceptions) and note down common strengths too. Type up your notes and share them with the class in the next lesson. Model editing a child's work by using the visualiser and try improving the work together. Once the children have read your whole-class feedback they can look at their own work and improve it.

Views about marking *are* changing. In 2016 Ofsted released a clarification document challenging the idea that they expect in-depth marking: 'Inspectors must not give the impression that marking needs to be undertaken in any particular format and to any particular degree of sophistication or detail.' (Harford, 2016)

The Workload Review concluded, 'If your current approach is unmanageable or disproportionate, stop [doing] it.' (Department for Education, 2016b) Spread the word: it is no longer about endless, in-depth notes on children's work. It's about effective feedback – the sort that will actually help children learn. If the last two comments you've left in Amber's book are all about using capital letters and full stops, complete this with a next step task for her to practise them. If two weeks later she still isn't using capital letters and full stops correctly, change your approach – stop setting it as a next step comment and find some time during the lesson to go through sentence punctuation with her.

If your school's policy demands 12 'next steps' a week, written in 19 different colours and adorned with sticky notes, stamps and stickers, it's time to have a conversation about marking in your school. You don't have to be in a leadership role to evoke change, but it does help. Whether it's at the next staff meeting or just during a casual discussion in the staffroom, don't be afraid to ask the question, 'Does anyone else think we could be marking differently?'

# Sharpening the saw

In his book, *The 7 Habits of Highly Effective People*, Stephen Covey (1999) outlines the behaviours and skills he believes necessary to lead a happy and successful life. It's a book worth reading if you have time but, in summary, Covey identifies the following as seven habits that highly effective people adopt:

1   Be proactive.
2   Begin with the end in mind.
3   Put first things first.
4   Think win/win.
5   Seek first to understand, then to be understood.
6   Synergise.
7   Sharpen the saw.

It is the seventh habit, sharpening the saw, that is the glue that holds the first six together. In his book, Covey describes the scenario of a person working feverishly to saw down a tree. He works for five hours solid and is absolutely exhausted. His friend suggests he takes a break for a few minutes to sharpen the saw as it would speed up the process of cutting down the tree. 'I don't have time to sharpen the saw!' the man replies. 'I'm too busy sawing.'

You get the idea. To be an effective leader you need to look after yourself: physically, socially, emotionally, spiritually. It's about improving yourself as much as it's about looking after yourself. It's an ongoing process of self-care and improvement; it's not something that can be done for six weeks of the year only to be neglected again in September. Covey suggests dedicating an hour a day to sharpening your saw, but if you can't manage that try just 30 minutes. If, like me, you find it impossible to fit anything other than work in between Monday and Friday, try booking a class. In 2013 I took Italian classes on Wednesday evenings. I paid for 15 lessons upfront, which I knew would prevent me from cancelling. It meant that every week I had one day when I had to be out of the door by 5pm at the latest. Dinners with friends I could cancel, calling my parents I could postpone, but a class that I'd booked and paid for was a real commitment and it got me out of the door on time every week.

Below are some suggestions of activities that would help you take care of your physical, mental, social and emotional health. Feel free to cross them out and add your own instead or jot down your own grid.

| Physical | Mental |
|---|---|
| - Attend an exercise class with a friend.<br>- Take an evening stroll.<br>- Cook a healthy meal.<br>- Find a new workout video on YouTube. | - Read anything. Just read.<br>- Write – whether it's a journal, a poem, an email (not a work email) or even just a letter.<br>- Learn a new skill (e.g. baking). |
| **Social/Emotional** | **Spiritual** |
| - Volunteer your time once a week.<br>- Phone a relative or friend you've recently neglected.<br>- Carry out a random act of kindness (e.g. pay for somebody's bus ticket or coffee). | - Reflect on your day (e.g. what went well?).<br>- Meditate.<br>- Keep a bullet journal (or a blog!).<br>- Practise mindfulness. |

You could be the most outstanding middle leader your school has ever had, but if you're always ill because you never take time to go to the doctor, you're not going to be able to do your job effectively. If you come back from the Easter holidays exhausted because you spent them working, you aren't going to be able to do your job effectively.

## Don't be a martyr

I became a teacher because I believed it was one of the most noble and important jobs you could do. I believed that spending 60 hours a week working was honourable and if I didn't do it I'd be 'letting the pupils down'. I spent hours doing unnecessary jobs: covering books, laminating resources that didn't require laminating, creating extra resources that didn't add any value to the lesson other than aesthetics. I remember once planning a lesson on complex sentences for Year 5. I'd come up with an activity that required the pupils to match the independent clause to the subordinating clause and copy it into their books. At about 6pm my headteacher walked in and found me stressing over the lesson.

'What's the problem with it?' she asked.

'It's just not interesting enough. At the moment all I'm going to do is explain what a complex sentence is, model how to write one and then send them to write the complex sentences in their books.'

'Well,' she replied, 'You *could* print and cut up the clauses and put them in envelopes on each table and then they could stick the clauses together to make sentences on sugar paper, but do you think they'll learn it any better than just by doing the work in their books?'

This was the first time someone had told me that a good lesson was good enough and that there isn't actually any correlation between the number of carefully cut-out resources you have and how much the pupils learn. After that I got into the habit of asking myself, '*Why* am I doing this?' and if the answer wasn't, 'Because it will help the pupils in my class learn', then I scrapped it. Sometimes good is good enough.

## Take a day off

Ideally not between Monday and Friday (although if you need to, do), but try to have one full day off a week. A day when you don't check emails, don't buy educational resources when you're out shopping, don't plan lessons, don't mark books and don't even talk about work. It's not easy to do and will take some discipline, but it will do you so much good to switch off from work for 24 hours each week. Book a day trip or make plans to spend the day with friends.

# Just say no!

Who knew the cast of *Grange Hill* had it right all along? 'No' is an incredibly powerful word and one we're not great at using in the UK. I used to be the member of staff who would agree to do anything – no task was too much to ask. Need a member of staff to lead an extra-curricular club? Sign me up. An extra member of staff needed for the PTA disco on Friday evening? I'd be there. Need someone to team teach with the NQT next week? Send them to me. I'd say yes to anything and everything and would work around the clock to make sure I got it all done. This would normally be OK for about half a term, as long as I worked 50 or 60 hours and gave up my lunch break, but after a few weeks I would start to feel as if I was sinking. It would always end up with me being unable to meet all my commitments but, rather than let people down at work, I let down my friends and family. I cancelled on friends last minute, never went to see either of my parents, and ducked out of as many social commitments as I could. It wasn't sustainable and it was making me (and my friends and family) miserable. I'd got it into my head that saying no was rude or would cause offence, but that isn't true. Saying no is a vital part of looking after your wellbeing. It doesn't have to be rude or abrupt, just something along the lines of, 'I'd love to help with that, but I've got enough on my plate as it is at the moment. I hope you find someone.'

If flat-out refusal still sounds too blunt, try this next time you're asked to do something extra: show them your to-do list and say, 'That's my family/me/exercising time, so if you want me to do that what should I cross off the list?' Phrasing it in that way puts the power back in the hands of the person asking the favour. It means you haven't refused them but you're asking them to assess whether you have the time to take on the extra work and, more often than not, they'll conclude from your list that you don't.

# Speak up

It is all too easy to dish out advice about managing workload and maintaining a work–life balance. The reality is there are times when work gets on top of everyone. Nobody is expecting you to be on top of everything all the time, so if you do find yourself struggling, for whatever reason, go and speak to somebody. My confidants are normally the other middle leaders – I go to them for advice or just to offload and we share ideas, tips and strategies. Whatever the problem, it is highly unlikely you are the first person to ever have dealt with it. Everyone has a to-do list they never get to the end of. If you're feeling overwhelmed by yours, ask to see your colleagues' lists – it'll help keep yours in perspective.

# Those who can Tweet

If you're already a 'tweacher' (a teacher with a Twitter account) then have a look at the hashtag #teacher5aday. #teacher5aday is an initiative that was set up by Martyn Reah (@MartynReah) to promote teacher wellbeing. The premise is simple enough: if teachers are happy the pupils will be happy. The initiative encourages teachers to write five pledges to themselves at the start of the school year. The pledges fall into the following categories: volunteer, connect, notice, learn and exercise. For some, these pledges take the form of a blog post and for others they are just a private journal entry. Over the course of the year, teachers take to social media to share their stress-busting tips and ideas. Twice a year there is a slow chat, which is a discussion over the course of five days on a specific topic, e.g. how to reduce planning and marking in schools. For me, I find having a network of teachers I can drop into for advice and support, any time day or night, invaluable.

But Twitter is not just good for wellbeing. Edutwitter, as tweachers call it, is where the latest developments in education are discussed, announcements from the Department for Education are fathomed out together and debates about pedagogy are thrashed out. Twitter introduced me to debates and ideas about teaching that I'd simply not heard being discussed at school and I'm a better teacher for it.

There are over half a million teachers in the UK. You may be struggling, overwhelmed or feeling as though you are drowning but the one thing you are not is alone.

# Promote wellbeing

I talked before about how taking Italian classes helped me leave work at a sociable hour once a week. However, it didn't just benefit me – once my colleagues heard I was taking an evening course it motivated them to take up a new hobby (one even signed up for the same course). When it comes to leading by example it doesn't just apply to classroom practice. Encourage your team to have interests and hobbies and take time to ask about them. 'How's the swimming going, Rachel? You've been doing that for a while now, haven't you?' Model that having a life outside of work is not just acceptable but to be encouraged.

Schools have got much better at promoting wellbeing in the last couple of years but it can sometimes feel slightly tokenistic (e.g. mental health champions, staff yoga lessons, cakes in the staffroom, locking up half an hour earlier). Locking up half an hour earlier doesn't reduce stress and often just means staff end up taking more work home with them. You end up sat in your lounge cutting out resources by hand for an hour – a job that would have taken ten minutes with the guillotine at school. And while cake and yoga are not bad things, the thing that is going to reduce staff stress better than any initiative is less work.

This means a conversation with the SLT and staff about what could be cut. Here are some changes I've seen made in schools recently that have made a real difference to workload. If they're happening in some schools, they can happen in all schools. I'm not suggesting you take this list to your headteacher and insist they make all these changes tomorrow, but use them to start the conversation by saying, 'I've got some ideas about reducing workload I'd like to share with you.'

- School reports reduced to one side of A4
- Data submitted once a term, not every six weeks
- No formal expectations on the number of 'next step comments' teachers should give pupils each week

- Bi-weekly staff meetings as opposed to weekly
- SLT release teachers for an hour every two weeks to give them time to feed back to children about their work
- Meetings to be no longer than an hour
- Staff have one 'duvet day' per academic year that they can cash in when they need a day off
- Scrapping formal planning

By just starting the conversation, you've taken a big step towards looking after your own wellbeing and that of your team.

# Chapter 11
# Your calendar

As I said in the previous chapter, managing your time is half the battle when you're a middle leader. Use this calendar to plot out your year, remembering to factor in the times of year when your class teacher hat will have to take priority over your middle leader hat (e.g. during the weeks of report writing). If you're finding it difficult to squeeze all your notes onto this page you can download a digital copy of the calendar at: www.bloomsbury.com/outstanding-middle-leader.

| Month | Task | Your notes |
|---|---|---|
| September | The start of a new school year is the perfect time to share your vision for your area of responsibility. (See Chapter 2.) | |
| October | You're now a month into the school year and you have some understanding of how the land lies. This may be the time to start thinking about drawing up an action plan. (See Chapter 3 for help.) | |
| November | By now the teachers will have had half a term with their new classes. This is a good time to get into classrooms and find out what's going on. (See Chapter 6.) | |

| December | It's the end of term. Have another look at your action plan and remind yourself of the targets you've set. What have you done this term to work towards them? What do your priorities for next term need to be? | |
|---|---|---|
| January | A headteacher once told me that the spring term is 'the Monday of the school year' – it's a very busy time. Start off the term by reminding everyone of your aims and vision – nothing formal just a quick chat in briefing will do! | |
| February | You're halfway through the school year! Now is a good time to have a look at the data. Does it throw up any interesting trends or gaps? (See Chapter 6 for help with analysing data.) | |
| March | Having looked at the data last month, March is a good time to do some observations and have another look at the books. Time to get triangulating. (See Chapter 7.) | |
| April | If you haven't done it already, now is a good time to do some pupil interviews. (For the sort of questions to ask and how to choose the children see Chapter 7.) | |
| May | May is generally assessment month. My advice would be to stay out of other people's classrooms. Let your class teacher hat take priority this month. | |

| June | June is a great month for monitoring. SATs are out of the way, teachers know their classes really well and end-of-year hysteria hasn't quite kicked in yet. | |
|------|------|------|
| July | The summer holidays are in sight, but there are still plenty of loose ends to tie up. Have one final look at the data for the year. Use your analysis and the evidence from your monitoring last month to start thinking about action plan targets for September. | |
| August | Relax. | |

# Glossary

I hope it was clear what each of these terms meant when you encountered them in the book, but if you're unsure, or just need a quick reminder, then you're in the right place.

**Academy** An academy is a state-funded school that is accountable to the Secretary of State for Education rather than the local authority.

**Achievement** An Ofsted judgement that takes into account both attainment and progress.

**Attainment** A pupil's grade, score or level.

**Book look** Taking a sample of children's work from each teacher to monitor teaching and learning.

**Community school** A non-faith, state-funded school that is accountable to the local authority.

**CP** Child protection.

**CPD** Continuing professional development, such as INSET, training or anything that helps staff develop their practice.

**EAL** English as an additional language.

**EYFS** Early Years Foundation Stage (this is both nursery and reception).

**Faith school** State-funded faith schools are usually voluntarily aided, which means they receive funding from a religious group or organisation (e.g. the Church of England). They are accountable to both the local authority and the diocese.

**Free school** A school that is state-funded but is run by a group or organisation.

**Formative assessment** Assessment that is done by the teacher to assess pupils' learning before and during a topic – it's generally not high-stakes testing and is used to inform the teacher's planning.

**FSM** Free school meals – this term is often used as a shorthand to refer to the pupils from low-income families who are eligible for free school meals (see also pupil premium).

**G&T** Gifted and talented pupils.

**HMI** Her Majesty's Inspectorate.

**Independent school** This is a fee-paying school that is not accountable to the local authority.

**INSET** In-service education and training.

**ISI** Independent Schools Inspectorate.

**KS1** Key Stage 1 (Years 1 and 2, 5–7 years old).

**KS2** Key Stage 2 (Years 3 to 6, 7–11 years old).

**LA** Local authority – the arm of the local council operation that deals and manages schools (apart from academies).

**LAC** Looked after children (children in care).

**National Expectations** The government's expectations of what pupils should attain nationally.

**NQT** Newly qualified teacher.

**PP** Pupil premium is additional funding to be used to raise the attainment of children from economically deprived backgrounds. Pupils receiving pupil premium funding are entitled to a free school meal (FSM) so they are sometimes referred to as FSM pupils.

**PPA** Planning, preparation and assessment time – this is release time that you are entitled to which is non-directed (you can't be told how to use it). It is the time to plan lessons, prepare resources, catch up on marking, etc.

**PPM** Pupil progress meeting – a termly meeting with the school leadership team to discuss the progress and attainment of pupils in your class.

**Progress** How much pupils' attainment has increased since the beginning of the year or key stage.

**PRP** Performance-related pay.

**RQT** Recently qualified teacher.

**SEF** School self-evaluation form – a document schools produce prior to an Ofsted inspection. The school evaluates the quality of the teaching, leadership, progress and attainment.

**SEN** Special educational needs.

**SIP** School improvement plan – a document that is produced on an annual basis outlining the school's priorities for the coming year. It is sometimes called a school development plan.

**SLT** Senior leadership team (sometimes referred to as the senior management team (SMT)).

**SPaG** Spelling, punctuation and grammar – this has become the informal name commonly used by teachers for the English grammar, punctuation and spelling test.

**Summative assessment** Assessment done at the end of a term or unit that is normally graded.

**TA** Teaching assistant.

**TLR** Teaching and learning responsibility – this refers to a member of staff who is responsible for the management of a subject, phase or year group. There are different levels of TLR from one to three and each has a different pay scale.

# Recommended reading

This list contains just some of the books that have got me through the last eight years of my career. You may not agree with everything they say, but they will make you think, they will challenge you and, ultimately, they will make you a better teacher and leader.

Berne, E. (1961), *Transactional Analysis in Psychotherapy: A Systematic Individual and Social Psychiatry*. Eastford: Martino Fine Books.

Buck, A. (2016), *Leadership Matters: How Leaders at All Levels Can Create Great Schools*. Woodbridge: John Catt Educational.

Christodoulou, D. (2017), *Making Good Progress? The Future of Assessment for Learning*. Oxford: Oxford University Press.

Cowley, S. (2014), *Getting the Buggers to Behave* (5th edn). London: Bloomsbury Education.

Crehan, L. (2018), *Cleverlands: The Secrets Behind the Success of the World's Education Superpowers*. London: Unbound.

de Board, R. (1997), *Counselling for Toads: A Psychological Adventure*. Abingdon: Routledge.

Gedge, N. (2016), *Inclusion for Primary School Teachers*. London: Bloomsbury Education.

Gill, S. (2018), *Successful Difficult Conversations in School: Improve Your Team's Performance, Behaviour and Attitude with Kindness and Success*. Woodbridge: John Catt Educational.

Harris, T. A. (2012), *I'm Ok – You're Ok*. London: Arrow.

Hendrik, C. (2017), *What Does This Look Like in the Classroom? Bridging the Gap Between Research and Practice*. Woodbridge: John Catt Educational.

Kell, E. (2018), *How to Survive in Teaching: Without Imploding, Exploding or Walking Away*. London: Bloomsbury Education.

Lucas, B. and Claxton, G. (2015), *Educating Ruby: What Our Children Really Need to Learn*. Carmarthen: Crown House Publishing.

McGill, R. M. (2017), *Mark. Plan. Teach.: Save Time. Reduce Workload. Impact Learning*. London: Bloomsbury Education.

Myatt, M. (2016), *High Challenge, Low Threat: How the Best Leaders Find Balance*. Woodbridge: John Catt Educational.

Tomsett, J. (2015), *This Much I Know About Love Over Fear: Creating a Culture of Truly Great Teaching*. Carmarthen: Crown House Publishing.

Wiliam, D. (2016), *Leadership for Teacher Learning: Creating a Culture Where All Teachers Improve So That All Students Succeed*. Bristol: Learning Science.

# Bibliography

Bell, D. and Ritchie, R. (1999), *Towards Effective Subject Leadership in the Primary School.* Milton Keynes: Open University Press.

Berne, E. (1961), *Transactional Analysis in Psychotherapy: A Systematic Individual and Social Psychiatry.* Eastford: Martino Fine Books.

Buck, A. (2016), *Leadership Matters: How Leaders at All Levels Can Create Great Schools.* Woodbridge: John Catt Educational.

Covey, S. (1999), *The 7 Habits of Highly Effective People.* London: Simon & Schuster.

Crystal, D. (2004), *Rediscover Grammar* (3rd edn). Harlow: Pearson.

Cuddy, A. (2012), 'Your body language may shape who you are', TED Talk, www.ted.com/talks/amy_cuddy_your_body_language_shapes_who_you_are

de Board, R. (1997), *Counselling for Toads: A Psychological Adventure.* Abingdon: Routledge.

Department for Education (2014), 'Number of schools, teachers and students in England', www.gov.uk/government/publications/number-of-schools-teachers-and-students-in-england

Department for Education (2016a), 'Initial teaching training: trainee number census – 2016–2017', www.gov.uk/government/statistics/initial-teacher-training-trainee-number-census-2016-to-2017

Department for Education (2016b), 'Eliminating unnecessary workload around marking', www.gov.uk/government/publications/reducing-teacher-workload-marking-policy-review-group-report

For Schools Education Service (2017), 'Key Stage 2 SATs national averages', www.forschoolseducation.co.uk/key-stage-2-sats-national-averages

Goetz, K. (2000), 'Perspectives on team teaching', http://people.ucalgary.ca/~egallery/goetz.html

Goleman, D. (2000), 'Leadership that gets results', *Harvard Business Review*, https://hbr.org/2000/03/leadership-that-gets-results

Harford, S. (2016), 'School inspection update: message to inspectors from the national director, education', www.ldbs.co.uk/wp-content/uploads/2017/01/2_185_school-inspection-update-november-2016.pdf

Hersey, P. and Blanchard, K. H. (1969), *Management of Organizational Behavior: Utilizing Human Resources.* Englewood Cliffs, NJ: Prentice Hall.

Jones, K. (2016), 'The work conversations we dread the most, according to research', *Harvard Business Review*, https://hbr.org/2016/04/the-work-conversations-we-dread-the-most-according-to-research

Murphy, R. (2013), 'Testing teachers', *Sutton Trust*, www.suttontrust.com/ wp-content/uploads/2013/03/MURPHYTEACHEREVALUATION-FINAL-1.pdf

National Governance Association (2018), 'Governance recruitment', www.nga. org.uk/Be-a-Governor.aspx

Newman, R., Furnham, A., Weis, L., Gee, M., Cardos, R., Lay, A. and McClelland, A. (2016), 'Non-verbal presence: how changing your behaviour can increase your ratings for persuasion, leadership and confidence', *Psychology*, 7, (4), 488–99.

Ofsted (2015), 'School inspection handbook', www.gov.uk/government/ publications/school-inspection-handbook-from-september-2015

Ofsted (2018), 'Ofsted inspections: myths', www.gov.uk/government/ publications/school-inspection-handbook-from-september-2015/ ofsted-inspections-mythbusting

Rowling, J. K. (2005), *Harry Potter and the Half-Blood Prince*. London: Bloomsbury.

Schmich, M. (1997), 'Advice, like youth, probably wasted on the young', *Chicago Tribune*, www.chicagotribune.com/news/columnists/chi-schmich-sunscreen-column-column.html

Scott, S. (2011), *Fierce Leadership: A Bold Alternative to the Worst 'Best Practices' of Business Today*. London: Piakus.

Sinek, S. (2011), *Start With Why: How Great Leaders Inspire Everyone to Take Action*. London: Penguin.

Smith, J. (2017), *The Lazy Teacher's Handbook: How Your Students Learn More When You Teach Less* (revised edn). Carmarthen: Crown House Publishing.

Toop, J. (2013), 'Making the most of middle leaders to drive change in schools', *The Guardian*, www.theguardian.com/teacher-network/teacher-blog/2013/ jul/02/middle-leaders-driving-change-school

Weale, S. (2015), 'Four in 10 new teachers quit within a year', *The Guardian*, www.theguardian.com/education/2015/mar/31/four-in-10-new-teachers-quit-within-a-year

Wright, T. (2012), 'Guide to mentoring', *ATL*, www.atl.org.uk/Images/ATL%20 Guide%20to%20mentoring%20(Nov%2012).pdf

# Index